INTERVENTIONS

Conor Cunningham and Peter Candler

GENERAL EDITORS

It's not a question of whether one believes in God or not. Rather, it's a question of if, in the absence of God, we can have belief, any belief.

"If you live today," wrote Flannery O'Connor, "you breathe in nihilism." Whether "religious" or "secular," it is "the very gas you breathe." Both within and without the academy, there is an air common to both deconstruction and scientism — both might be described as species of *reductionism.* The dominance of these modes of knowledge in popular and professional discourse is quite incontestable, perhaps no more so where questions of theological import are often subjugated to the margins of intellectual respectability. Yet it is precisely the proponents and defenders of religious belief in an age of nihilism that are often among those most — unwittingly or not — complicit in this very reduction. In these latter cases, one frequently spies an accommodationist impulse, whereby our concepts must be first submitted to a prior philosophical court of appeal in order for them to render any intellectual value. To cite one particularly salient example, debates over the origins, nature, and ends of human life are routinely partitioned off into categories of "evolutionism" and "creationism," often with little nuance. Where attempts to mediate these arguments are to be found, frequently the strategy is that of a kind of accommodation: How can we adapt our belief in creation to an already established evolutionary metaphysic, or, how can we have our evolutionary cake and eat it too? It is sadly the case that, despite the best intentions of such "intellectual ecumenism," the distinctive voice of theology is the first one to succumb to aphony — either from impetuous overuse or from a deliberate silencing.

The books in this unique new series propose no such simple accommodation. They rather seek and perform tactical interventions in such debates in a manner that problematizes the accepted terms of such debates. They propose something altogether more demanding: through a kind of refusal of the disciplinary isolation now standard in modern universities, a genuinely interdisciplinary series of mediations of crucial concepts and key figures in contemporary thought. These volumes will attempt to discuss these topics as they are articulated within their own field, including their historical emergence, and cultural significance, which will provide a way into seemingly abstract discussions. At the same time, they aim to analyze what consequences such thinking may have for theology, both positive and negative, and, in light of these new perspectives, to develop an effective response — one that will better situate students of theology and professional theologians alike within the most vital debates informing Western society, and so increase their understanding of, participation in, and contribution to these.

To a generation brought up on a diet of deconstruction, on the one hand, and scientism, on the other, Interventions offers an alternative that is *otherwise than nihilistic* — doing so by approaching well-worn questions and topics, as well as historical and contemporary figures, from an original and interdisciplinary angle, and so avoid having to steer a course between the aforementioned Scylla and Charybdis.

This series will also seek to navigate not just through these twin dangers, but also through the dangerous "and" that joins them. That is to say, it will attempt to be genuinely interdisciplinary in avoiding the conjunctive approach to such topics that takes as paradigmatic a relationship of "theology and phenomenology" or "religion and science." Instead, the volumes in this series will, in general, attempt to treat such discourses not as discrete disciplines unto themselves, but as moments within a distended theological performance. Above all, they will hopefully contribute to a renewed atmosphere shared by theologians and philosophers (not to mention those in other disciplines) — an air that is not nothing.

CENTRE OF THEOLOGY AND PHILOSOPHY

(www.theologyphilosophycentre.co.uk)

Every doctrine which does not reach the one thing necessary, every separated philosophy, will remain deceived by false appearances. It will be a doctrine, it will not be Philosophy.

Maurice Blondel, 1861-1949

This book series is the product of the work carried out at the Centre of Theology and Philosophy (COTP), at the University of Nottingham.

The COTP is a research-led institution organized at the interstices of theology and philosophy. It is founded on the conviction that these two disciplines cannot be adequately understood or further developed, save with reference to each other. This is true in historical terms, since we cannot comprehend our Western cultural legacy unless we acknowledge the interaction of the Hebraic and Hellenic traditions. It is also true conceptually, since reasoning is not fully separable from faith and hope, or conceptual reflection from revelatory disclosure. The reverse also holds, in either case.

The Centre is concerned with:

- the historical interaction between theology and philosophy.
- the current relation between the two disciplines.
- attempts to overcome the analytic/continental divide in philosophy.
- the question of the status of "metaphysics": Is the term used equivocally? Is it now at an end? Or have twentieth-century attempts to have a postmetaphysical philosophy themselves come to an end?
- the construction of a rich Catholic humanism.

I am very glad to be associated with the endeavours of this extremely important Centre that helps to further work of enormous importance. Among its concerns is the question whether modernity is more an interim than a completion — an interim between a premodernity in which the porosity between theology and philosophy was granted, perhaps taken for granted, and a postmodernity where their porosity must be unclogged and enacted anew. Through the work of leading theologians of international stature and philosophers whose writings bear on this porosity, the Centre offers an exciting forum to advance in diverse ways this challenging and entirely needful, and cutting-edge work.

Professor William Desmond, Leuven

WORDS OF CHRIST

Michel Henry

Translated by

Christina M. Gschwandtner

Foreword by

Jean-Yves Lacoste

Introduction by

Karl Hefty

WILLIAM B. EERDMANS PUBLISHING COMPANY

GRAND RAPIDS, MICHIGAN / CAMBRIDGE, U.K.

Originally published in French as *Paroles du Christ*
© 2002 Éditions du Seuil

English translation © 2012 Wm. B. Eerdmans Publishing Co.
All rights reserved

Published 2012 by
Wm. B. Eerdmans Publishing Co.
2140 Oak Industrial Drive N.E., Grand Rapids, Michigan 49505 /
P.O. Box 163, Cambridge CB3 9PU U.K.
www.eerdmans.com

Printed in the United States of America

16 15 14 13 12   7 6 5 4 3 2 1

Library of Congress Cataloging-in-Publication Data

Henry, Michel, 1922-2002.
[Paroles du Christ. English]
Words of Christ / Michel Henry; translated by Christina M. Gschwandtner.
p.   cm.   — (Interventions)
ISBN 978-0-8028-6288-4 (cloth: alk. paper)
1. Jesus Christ — Words.   2. Word of God (Christian theology)
3. Phenomenological theology.   I. Title.

BT306.H26713   2012
232.9'54 — dc23

2011039631

Contents

CONTENTS

Foreword

Jean-Yves Lacoste

From *Philosophie et phénoménologie du corps*[1] — the first book he wrote, before *L'Essence de la manifestation* — to *Paroles du Christ*,[2] the intellectual itinerary of Michel Henry followed a straight line. This was due to a love and an uncompromising search for truth. It was also due (his readers should be aware) to the deepening *(approfondissement)* of a field of reality, "life's" own. For Henry, the meaning of "life" is not biological. According to the philosopher, who was probably the most anti-Heideggerian of all the phenomenologists, life is primarily an anti-ecstasy or, we might say, non-existence. For Heidegger, existence is defined as an essential being-outside-of-oneself. That which exists is perpetually ahead of itself, in concern, in solicitude, in anticipatory resoluteness, and in other phenomena. By contrast, life, for Henry, is the most interior of interiorities, the most immanent kind of immanence. Thus life has no world; it is not "in" any-

1. Completed in 1950, and published later (*Philosophie et phénoménologie du corps. Essai sur l'ontologie biranienne* (Paris: Presses Universitaires de France, 1965) [ET *Philosophy and Phenomenology of the Body,* trans. Girard Etzkorn (The Hague: Nijhoff, 1975)], two years after *L'Essence de la manifestation,* 2 vols. (Paris: Presses Universitaires de France, 1963) [ET *The Essence of Manifestation,* trans. Girard Etzkorn (The Hague: Nijhoff, 1973)].
   2. (Paris: Editions du Seuil, 2002).

thing. Rather, life experiences itself in affective experience, to the point of affecting itself and, as Henry likes to say, "embracing" itself. The privileged phenomena are thus pain and joy, understood as non-intentional acts. Pain is not pain-of, joy is not joy-of — they are most fundamentally life's self-revelation feeling itself in pain or joy. A consequence follows from this. The proposed interpretation of the non-existent phenomenon of life brackets any interpretation of death and, above all, of a being-towards-death: life is always living now. The now in which life embraces itself is "moving" *(pathétique),* affected and felt; but no future looms above it and no past exerts control over it. Life is lived in the present.

This book, a posthumous publication of a manuscript that Henry had written and reviewed in its entirety, also speaks of life. Here, however, it speaks of life in the register of theology and, at root, of spirituality: life has become Life. The author tells us that life, as conceptualized in more "rigorously" philosophical works, cannot give itself to itself. If there is such a thing as life, and if life cannot give itself to itself, the reason we are offered is no mystery at all: (human) life is engendered by a divine Life. Life / life, l / L: this subtle orthographic shift does not indicate a theological "turn"; rather, it quite simply points out to phenomenology that, when it concerns itself with the words (and works) of Christ, it finally arrives at the arch-phenomenon that gives meaning to all other phenomena. In the light of Life, life realizes its highest possibilities. Those possibilities were not unknown to Henry, and forty years of philosophical work were dedicated to their exploration. In the works up to *C'est moi la vérité*[3] — which marks the philosopher's resolute commitment to Christianity — life occurs within the order of fact and fact alone. It is not until *Paroles du Christ* that facticity reveals, in addition to its own logic, the ultimate laws that govern it. In thinking Life, Henry thinks life in its foundation. And the foundation of life is divine. The one who lives is not one who exists. In these final pages of Henry, we learn that life is a daughter of God.

Translated by AARON RICHES *and* PETER M. CANDLER JR.

---

3. *C'est moi la vérité. pour une philosophie du christianisme* (Paris: Editions du Seuil, 1996) [ET *I Am the Truth: Toward a Philosophy of Christianity,* trans. Susan Emanuel (Stanford, CA: Stanford University Press, 2003)].

Introduction to the English Edition

Words of Christ brings to completion the philosophical and literary work of Michel Henry, one of the leading philosophers in Europe during the latter half of the twentieth century. He finished the revisions of its manuscript while in a hospital in Albi, France, shortly before his death on July 3, 2002. Published in October of that year and offered here in English translation for the first time, this book proposes a new approach to the question of the legitimacy and justification of the words of Jesus, to the determination of their meaning and the intelligibility of their content. Insofar as these words bear upon the mystery of his person, the unavoidable question of his divinity is also posed, and answered, in this book.

Henry's *Words of Christ* concludes a triptych of books devoted to the question of Christianity, a major focus of his work from the early 1990s. At the same time, it presents the final articulation of a new philosophy of language, whose initial contours appear in inchoate form in his writings from the 1940s, but which also had become an explicit project during the last decade of his life. Above all, this book marks the culmination of a lifelong effort to articulate a phenomenologically adequate concept of self-revelation, which in this book means Revelation, Scripture, and ultimately the Word of God. Uniting and summarizing these philosophical projects, each significant in its own right, *Words of Christ* poses the question of what these words mean for humanity, for its understanding of itself, the possibility of its salvation but also of its destruction.

For much of contemporary philosophy and culture, questions of this sort have been considered out of bounds, beyond the limits of what can and cannot be said with reason, articles of faith, at best, at worst unintelligible. But *Words of Christ* does not depend upon the resources of historical or textual criticism to demonstrate any specific meaning that may or may not be deciphered in the words of Jesus. It investigates the speech of Jesus starting from a different set of premises, which answer to a truly fundamental problem. What determines human existence to be what it is? What makes each of us who we are, and what means lay at our disposal to answer this question? No one living can avoid giving an answer, even less so when the question has not been posed. When he was a young man barely in his twenties, a member of the French Resistance amid the devastation of a world at war, Henry began to grasp this problem and its importance.[1] It would direct the course and development of his philosophy for the next six decades.

At the outset of his work, Henry framed the fundamental theme of his philosophy in terms of a phenomenology of the ego. He approached this problem initially through the conceptual means supplied by Husserl and Heidegger, whose philosophy had been recently introduced in France; but he gradually concluded that their resources proved inadequate to the task. Referring to his first major work, *The Essence of Manifestation,* which he composed over the course of the 1950s, Henry writes: "This book was born of a refusal, the refusal of the very philosophy from which it has sprung. . . . [T]he very concepts which we rejected were the ones that guided the problem initially. . . . [T]his book is dedicated to the clarification of the secret essence of our being which, at the end of the phenomenological process of analysis, will prove to be nothing other than affectivity."[2] The great theme of Henry's philosophy, and in one sense the only theme, is that affectivity is not merely content, but also a

1. In a journal kept during World War II, Henry noted in 1945, "Husserl's conception of regional ontologies is one of the best refutations of nihilism, better than the philosophy of St. Thomas or Aristotle, for it is no longer only essences that have an essence, but existence does as well. And existence can have jurisdiction over the essences, can level them, can de-realize them, can make every appearance a *sub specie* of nothing. This stops with Husserl." Cited by Jean Leclercq, "Biographie de Michel Henry," in *Michel Henry. Pour une phénoménologie de la vie* (Clichy: Editions du Corlevour, 2010), p. 12.

2. From the 1972 "Author's Preface" to the English translation, *The Essence of Manifestation,* trans. Girard Etzkorn (The Hague: Martinus Nijhoff, 1973), pp. xi, xii.

form, indeed *the* fundamental form, of pure phenomenality. Human existence acquires concrete determination neither through the concept nor through the principle of identity, nor through reference to the horizon of being in general, but only through affectivity.

In the philosophy of Husserl and Heidegger, phenomenality refers to originary transcendence. The things that show themselves in consciousness are nevertheless in an outside, by virtue of the very acts through which the mind intends its objects. If human existence begins only after first being in the world, any serious understanding of who we are will always require opposition to that world for its very possibility. In either case, the manner in which subjectivity acquires concrete character presupposes a distance, to which it refers and on which it depends for its own determination. This distance is phenomenological in the sense that the effective appearing of subjectivity not only refers to the appearing of the world but also borrows its meaning from it.[3] An unbridgeable distance separates what shows itself from the way that it does so. But if subjectivity has concrete character, this subjectivity does not show itself in the same way that the world does. As Kant implicitly recognized, if the transcendence that characterizes the world is the only modality of appearing, then subjectivity is quite literally unthinkable, and the world is, too.

Against this unilateral approach, Henry's philosophy is devoted to defining and explaining another mode of phenomenality, one that is original and absolute, and on which the phenomenality of the world itself depends. He defines this mode of appearing as self-affection, a term which he borrows from Kant and Heidegger, but to which he assigns a different meaning. For them the subject is affected by itself in the same way that it is affected by the world. But Henry maintains that the subject cannot be determined first by reference to a content foreign to it. Not only would it feel itself first as foreign, but this alienation would then define it irremediably. But even this supposed distance from oneself presupposes that the subject is first affected by its own content, by itself. Henry calls this original affection of oneself "ipseity," the simple fact of

---

3. Michel Henry, *L'essence de la manifestation* (Paris: Presses Universitaires de France, 1st ed. 1963, 3rd ed. 2003), §31, pp. 289ff. *The Essence of Manifestation*, § 9, pp. 59ff.

being oneself.[4] For this way of appearing, defined by self-affection, he reserves the name "life." And insofar as the appearing of the world depends upon life, only one of these irreducible modes of appearing is absolute.

A phenomenological determination of the ego is finally possible, since only because life is given to itself in self-affection is it possible to say "I" or "me" or to perform any act at all, linguistic, mental, and even corporeal, without absurdity. The *cogitatio,* the possibility of thinking or willing, for example, of wanting or not wanting, indeed of loving, all these have coherence, concrete integrity, and real meaning only in and through life's affectivity. All human action of any sort borrows its power and effectiveness from life. For this reason alone action is meaningful. But for the same reason, it is impossible in principle to determine one's being or identity by one's action, since it is impossible to determine one's affection by one's action. The source and possibility of human existence does not depend on the power of the ego, but on the life that gives it this power.

If God is life, then the manner of determining the relationship of humanity and God has been entirely transformed. Because life is phenomenological, it is inescapably concrete. Our relation to ourselves, or rather our being ourselves, depends first on life, which cannot be attained by an action any more than we ourselves can.[5] Only in the absolute passivity of the self-affection that gives it to itself is the ego a self at all. Only there is its life intelligible. Henry finds in the preaching of Meister Eckhart resources that enable him to confirm and develop this notion of ipseity in terms of self-revelation. Self-revelation performs its work only in humility and poverty, in the absence of any appeal to property or accomplishment, real or imagined. If God is life, in all of its concrete actuality, the self-revelation of life is God's own self-revelation. For Eckhart, as for Henry, *this* self-revelation performs its work only in humility and poverty, in the absence of any appeal to property or accomplishment, real or imagined. We find its succinct expression in Eckhart's Sermon 6, which Henry cites often: "God engenders himself as myself."[6]

---

4. *L'essence de la manifestation,* §31, pp. 289ff.; ET, pp. 234ff.

5. *L'essence de la manifestation,* §§68-69, pp. 803ff.; ET, pp. 642ff.

6. Michel Henry, "Phénoménologie de la vie," in *Phénoménologie de la vie,* vol. 1: *De la*

In the three decades after 1960, Henry began to show the fecundity of his thesis on the duplicity of appearing by applying it to certain fundamental problems in philosophy. In the late 1940s, in a work initially conceived as the first chapter of *The Essence of Manifestation* but which amounts to a first application of its thesis, he developed an original account of the human body. Through a novel interpretation of the thought of Maine de Biran, Kant's near contemporary who was in the 1940s still a relatively unknown figure, Henry showed that the duality of appearing makes the human body intelligible in a way unknown to classical or modern philosophy. The body is given to us twice, so to speak.[7] It appears as an object in the world that can be seen and touched, but it also appears to itself in a subjective unity that is invisible, and endowed with the original power of sensing, and thus also touching and seeing. The body is not first an empirical object in the world. The body is first subjective.

The unity of these two modes of appearing gains concrete character in the body. Only on the basis of this original ontological unity is knowledge of the world possible. However, the unity of the subjective body is not an ideal unity. It is not an empty logical principle of identity, but the concrete unity of the subjective body. Because the body is subjective, it is possible to determine the categories of logic in an entirely new way. Not only does unity have real meaning, but so does causality, and difference, and quality, and the other categories of thought that make knowledge of the world possible. More importantly, the subjective body sheds new light upon Henry's original question about the meaning of humanity, about what makes each of us who we are. For many philosophers and for popular opinion alike, the ability to think defines human existence. But reason itself, the coherence of a thought, is possible only because the body is subjective. The relation of thought to life thus acquires new

phénoménologie (Paris: Presses Universitaire de France, 2003), p. 69; citing Meister Eckhart, "Sermon No. 6," in *Traités et sermons* (Paris: Aubier, 1942), p. 146. See *Meister Eckhart: The Essential Sermons, Commentaries, Treatises, and Defense,* trans. Edmund Colledge and Bernard McGinn (Mahwah, NJ: Paulist Press, 1981), p. 187.

7. Michel Henry, *Philosophie et phénoménologie du corps* (Paris: Presses Universitaires de France, 1st ed. 1965, 5th ed. 2003), p. 160; ET: *Philosophy and Phenomenology of the Body,* trans. Girard Etzkorn (The Hague: Martinus Nijhoff, 1975), p. 115.

meaning: "If the categories are founded in our life, it is because what we think depends upon what we are."[8]

Already at this early stage in his career, Henry saw that the discovery of the subjective body also required a new approach to language. Like appearing itself, the signifying character of language is also double. "The sign which draws its entire meaning from the internal transcendental experience of our original body can, nevertheless, equally refer to the natural being of the objective body."[9] This twofold usage of signs makes the peculiar character of human language intelligible — not only the possibility of speaking truth, but also the possibility of duplicity and falsehood. In the approach to language suggested here, we see an early indication of the philosophy of language that Henry will articulate more than thirty years later, culminating in *Words of Christ*. But his early treatment of the problem did not go unnoticed. Shortly after his habilitation, Henry received an admiring letter and two articles from a young philosopher named Jacques Derrida, who several years later would publish a number of books on language, including *Speech and Phenomenon* and *Writing and Difference*.[10]

In 1960 Henry turned down the first of several offers of a tenured position in philosophy at the University of Paris, in favor of a position in Montpellier, near the Mediterranean coast. He would teach there until his retirement in 1982. The next decades would afford him the occasion to deepen his phenomenology of life and to extend it in new directions. In the mid-1960s, the educational system required him to teach Marx for the aggregation. Much to his surprise, he discovered in Marx a philosopher of extreme genius, whom he would later describe as "the Aristotle of modern times."[11] But in his view, the original ideas of Marx had virtually nothing in common with Marxist ideology; yet that interpretation had determined the reception of Marx for decades. Henry found himself compelled to spend the next ten years working out a completely new in-

8. *Philosophie et phénoménologie du corps*, p. 102; ET, p. 74.

9. *Philosophie et phénoménologie du corps*, p. 186; ET, p. 134.

10. Jean Leclercq and Anne Henry, "Entretien en manière de biographie," in *Dossier Michel Henry* (Lausanne: Editions L'Age d'Homme, 2009), p. 29.

11. Interview with Bogdan Mihai Mandache, *Cronica*, October 1992. Reprinted in Michel Henry, *Entretiens* (Arles: Sulliver, 2005), p. 92.

terpretation of Marx's philosophy, one contrary to the prevailing Marxist doctrine.[12] This new interpretation was made possible, in part, by close attention to the *1844 Manuscripts* and the *German Ideology,* which had been discovered only in 1932, long after the principal tenants of Marxism had been constituted.

The rediscovery of Marx is important insofar as it provides a means for Henry to answer not only the question of what makes us who we are but also how it is possible that we are capable of producing real things, and the difficulty in principle of assigning value to them. Real human production is possible only because it is first concrete and living, not because it has been determined first through an abstract or theoretical idea. For Marx, on Henry's reading, "it is praxis, individual effort, the activity of an organic subjectivity, which are at the basis of everything."[13] The appropriation of Marx by socialism thus depends on a fundamental misunderstanding of his thought, one that ignores his philosophy of the concrete individual. But Henry's reinterpretation of the essence of living labor also overturns a basic premise of capitalism. It explains the impossibility in principle of exchanging any objective equivalent for living subjective labor, a labor whose "division" itself depends upon this exchange. If human labor constitutes an essential dimension of human existence, then it is irreducible, of absolute value, and cannot be measured.[14] If the source of value consists in living labor, the gradual effort to lower "costs" by eliminating human labor from the means of production must ultimately eliminate any possibility of value or of profit. Although controversial at the time and still largely unknown in the English-speaking world, Henry's interpretation of Marx sees in him a great philosopher, and one whose ideas were distorted not only by socialism, but also by Marxism as such.

Beyond this explanation of the concrete character of human produc-

12. Michel Henry, *Marx I. Une philosophie de la réalité, Marx II. Une philosophie de l'économie* (Paris: Gallimard, 1976); ET: *Marx: A Philosophy of Reality* (Bloomington: Indiana University Press, 1983).

13. "Que l'individu soit rendu à lui-même," interview with Roger Pol Droit, *Le Monde,* April 16, 1976. Reprinted in Henry, *Entretiens,* p. 27.

14. Interview with Thierry Galibert, *Autre Sud,* December 11, 2000. Reprinted in Henry, *Entretiens,* pp. 124, 125.

tion, the phenomenology of life also sheds light on other domains. It clarifies the peculiar relationship between modern science and modern culture. To be more precise, it explains why modern science renders human life unintelligible. Science renders human life unintelligible for no other reason than because it excludes what is human from its field of vision. This exclusion begins when modern science begins, when Galileo eliminates all subjective qualities from the definition of what is real. No longer capable of considering colors, sounds, and other specifically human qualities, the conception of science that ensues deals only with objective determinations, such as shape, form, figure, and extension. And it treats these determinations in abstraction from the real and living subjective body they nevertheless always presuppose. For Henry, this decision portends the demise of human culture and the inevitable colonization of science by technology, which we all witness today. "To remove sensible qualities from the reality of objects is to eliminate our sensibility at the same time, the ensemble of our impressions, emotions, desires and passions, of our thoughts, in brief, our entire subjectivity which makes up the substance of our life. . . . The kiss lovers exchange is only a bombardment of microphysical particles."[15] If culture finds its source in life and its modalities, the domination of this science coincides with the demise of culture, in all its forms. The naive dependence upon science as the sole means of access to ourselves, to who and what we are, means only that we no longer know who we are.

The duplicity of phenomenality not only brings clarity to the defining theoretical decisions that determine the contemporary world as a world of science; it also shines new light on art, its place in the life of human culture, and the possibility of its renewal. For Henry, who was unusually well acquainted with the history of art, and above all with the history of painting, the essence of art is life. For a dominant strain of Western art, painting means painting the world, and therefore borrowing its means and manners of showing from the world, with the goal of presenting it again, perhaps in a new light. Strongly antithetical to this idea, the phenomenology of life renders the principles of aesthetics intel-

---

15. Michel Henry, "Preface" (dated October 2000), for the "Quadrige" edition, *La Barbarie*, 2nd ed. (Paris: Presses Universitaires de France, 2004), p. 2.

ligible in a new way. The real subject of a painting is invisible, not in the world. It is not a copy of a model, but the original. For this reason, what art shows, or rather what shows itself in art, is life.[16] "The Life and real being of a work, which seem to be there, in the outside, are in me. . . . A phenomenology of exteriority is incapable of defining an aesthetic."[17]

If the essence of art is life, the criteria for aesthetic judgment have nothing to do with the success or failure of a work in representing an object in the world. They consist in the power of a work of art to increase sensibility and sensitivity to life, which it can do only on the basis of a knowledge. Insofar as art shows humanity to itself, the rise and fall of human culture is linked to that of art. For this reason, according to Henry, art is also inseparable from ethics, which it expresses in a higher form. A culture whose sensitivity is dulled to life is inevitably an unethical culture, since the first principles of ethics are drawn from the needs of life, for food, clothing, shelter, work. Where these needs go unmet, culture itself cannot fully develop. If religion concerns the relation of men and women to the life of God, and therefore consists in the knowledge and the practice that brings humanity back to life, art itself is also, in an essential way, religious.[18]

Henry devoted the last decade of his life to the question of Christianity, and this work produced a sequence of three major books, which concludes with *Words of Christ*. It was in rereading the texts of John and Paul that he discovered what he would come to regard as another phenomenology of life, one more ancient and more direct than his own. The first of these works, *I Am the Truth: Toward a Philosophy of Christianity*, considers the Christian conception of truth in light of the phenomenology of life. This approach, though never abandoned, would nevertheless later require a reversal of phenomenology itself, to the point that phenomenology can no longer proceed by interpreting Christianity under its own light, but only under the light of a more fundamental Revelation. Both

16. Michel Henry, *Voir l'invisible. Sur Kandinsky* (1st ed. Paris: Editions François Bourin, 1988; 2nd ed. Paris: Presses Universitaires de France, 2005), pp. 205-9.

17. Interview with Olivier Salazar-Ferrer, *Agone*, 4th trimester, 1991. Reprinted in Henry, *Entretiens*, p. 67.

18. Michel Henry, "Art et phénoménologie de la vie," in *Phénoménologie de la vie*, vol. 3: *De l'art et du politique* (Paris: Presses Universitaire de France, 2004), pp. 297ff.

phenomenology and Christianity share this Revelation as their common source, and both presume it, though in distinct ways. Henry in no way seeks to reduce Christianity to a phenomenology of life. On the contrary, he finds of interest in the texts of Christianity precisely their power to express what philosophy cannot.

Henry's initial set of questions related to Christianity concern its definition of truth, and specifically the manner in which this truth is *not* founded on logic. Truth in the logical sense consists first in an empty and ideal form that only then is available to be satisfied or not satisfied by a content; but truth in the Christian sense means life, and the characteristic of this life is that it always engenders a living. The truth of the relationship between life and living is not an abstract equality of identity, A = A, nor the relation between essence and existence, but the real phenomenological content of a real and concrete unity. As he puts it, "No life without living. No living without life."[19]

The reciprocal relationship between life and living provides a means of understanding why the Gospel of John calls Christ the Firstborn Son. The Firstborn Son, capitalized because it is a proper name, is unique and original in the sense that he is the living proper to the invisible life of God. For Henry, this interior reciprocal relationship between Life and the First Living expresses in phenomenological terms what Christianity expresses in another way when it identifies Christ with the truth. It is this account of truth that we will also see Henry develop and extend in *Words of Christ.* The emphasis on Christ's interior relationship with his Father in no way devalues his historical existence. On the contrary, it renders it intelligible, since only his relationship with the Father determines his historical existence from beginning to end.

As Henry works through the encounter between the phenomenology of life and Christianity, a new question about human finitude emerges. If we are incapable of giving life to ourselves, how do we come into our condition as living? Each and every living can be living only through the work of life in it. But what distinguishes each of us as living

19. Michel Henry, *C'est moi, la vérité* (Paris: Seuil, 1996), p. 80; ET: *I Am the Truth: Toward a Philosophy of Christianity,* trans. Susan Emanuel (Stanford: Stanford University Press, 2003), p. 60.

from the Christ, if he is the unique First Living? Nothing but our power-lessness with regard to the condition that defines us. The self-affection that constitutes my life is not my doing. "I do not affect myself absolutely, but, precisely put, I am and I find myself self-affected."[20]

Nevertheless, each of us is defined by our condition as sons and daughters. In the end, for Henry, this is the only adequate definition of humanity. Only on the basis of this condition and in light of it do the par-adoxical injunctions that define Christian ethics become intelligible and coherent, though in purely logical terms they remain contradictory. One's actions lead either to salvation or to perdition, for example, and yet no one can decide his or her fate by an action.[21] Although our condition can be forgotten, it cannot be destroyed. And insofar as the possibility of salvation is rooted in it, this salvation can be defined as the restoration of an original condition.

Certain theologians initially criticized *I Am the Truth* for tending in a Gnostic direction by effacing the corporal dimension of Christianity, but in Henry's view these criticisms ignored or were unaware of the fact that he had first rewritten the philosophy of the body. Nevertheless, the confronta-tion with Christianity did compel him, in a second book, to pose at a deeper level the problem of the body. This new inquiry runs deeper in the sense that it is no longer merely a phenomenological determination of the flesh, of the body as living and subjective, but of the concrete manner in which life comes into the flesh. This set of problems does concern the phe-nomenology of the ego, or self, or me, but treats this question in terms of what comes before these determinations and makes them possible.

In order to address this question, Henry ultimately came to see a new approach as necessary, and he calls this approach the phenomenol-ogy of incarnation. What comes before each living (and thus before sub-jectivity) is already at work within each living. Within the living, absolute life is present and comes before each living in the sense that it gives it to itself. The phenomenological question then becomes the following: How does this "before" show itself? The point of departure for phenomenol-ogy cannot be some invented or fictitious life, one which we might imag-

20. *C'est moi, la vérité*, p. 136; ET, p. 107.
21. *C'est moi, la vérité*, p. 212; ET, p. 168.

ine or hope to be our own. Rather, the point of departure must arise "within the very process of life's self generation."[22] The self-givenness that constitutes your ipseity and mine must first be shown from within that process, since none of us can produce it for ourselves. Because a finite flesh is unable to give life to itself, each of us can be who we are as finite only through the incarnation of infinite life in us. The human condition is such that "our life is a finite life and, precisely to this extent, is an infinite life."[23]

Henry's treatment of the problem of finitude gives a new inflection to his philosophy, with implications for the relationship between phenomenology and theology. The phenomenology of life is not an artificial philosophical veneer placed over the doctrinal corpus of Christianity. Nor does it understand itself in any way to supersede Christianity. His approach is not, strictly speaking, a phenomenology of Christianity. Nor, on the other hand, does it presuppose an appropriation of Christian categories by phenomenology. Rather, it raises the bar of intelligibility to a new level, which both phenomenology and Christianity presuppose, and which Henry calls Arch-Revelation. "Here the phenomenological intuitions of Life and those of Christian theology meet: *in the recognition of a common presupposition which is no longer thought's own*. Before thought, thus before phenomenology and theology alike (before philosophy or any other theoretical discipline), a Revelation is at work, which owes them nothing, but which both equally presuppose."[24]

The remarkable character of this approach is not merely the manner in which it remains within a field of intelligibility, and to this extent within philosophy. The approach is remarkable because it restores to incarnation a more fundamental principle of intelligibility, all the while depending upon that intelligibility for its own. This restoration amounts to a repetition of the early doctrinal history of Christianity itself. The Judeo-Christian confrontation with Greek philosophy, on Henry's view, is a conflict between two modalities of phenomenality, between two competing conceptions of revelation. If the Christian apologists of the first

---

22. Michel Henry, *Incarnation. Une philosophie de la chair* (Paris: Seuil, 2000), p. 244.

23. Interview with Virginie Caruana, *Philosophique*, January 2000. Reprinted in Henry, *Entretiens*, p. 122. Interview with Thierry Galibert, p. 140.

24. Henry, *Incarnation*, p. 364.

centuries and the early councils of the church adopt Greek terms in order to articulate their faith, they do so only by evacuating them of their
Greek meaning, by refusing to reduce the revealing power of the incarnation to that of reason, or to understand this incarnation with conceptual
resources that presuppose a dualistic theory of the human being.[25] In
this sense, one might say, with *Words of Christ* in view, that the Judeo-
Christian confrontation with the world restores meaning to its language.

For this reason, one would be mistaken to interpret Henry's approach to Greek philosophy as one-sided, if the restoration the incarnation enacts is inseparable from the language in which it articulates itself.
From Henry's perspective, philosophy itself is at stake in this articulation: "The object of philosophy and that of religion are identical. . . . Our
culture proceeds from two sources: a Greco-Latin source and a Judeo-
Christian source, two profoundly different forms of thought, but which
have nevertheless united. Two streams have mixed their waters, even if
one comes from a plain and the other from a mountain. We are the children of this paradoxical and yet infinitely precious alliance, which must
not be lost. I fight for that, I'm not someone who lives in an ivory
tower."[26]

Before we consider *Words of Christ* in closer detail, we must first notice that, even before beginning to treat the question of Christianity directly, Henry from the early 1990s had already begun to work out a new
philosophy of language.[27] If the phenomenality of language depends
upon the phenomenality of life, then the way the truth of language shows
itself depends upon life and the way it shows itself. For this reason, "if ap-

25. Cf. Henry, *Incarnation*, pp. 16ff.
26. Interview with Thierry Galibert, p. 131.
27. "Parole et Religion. Parole de Dieu," originally presented May 15, 1992, at the École
normale supérieure, and published in *Phénoménologie et Théologie*, ed. J. F. Courtine
(Paris: Criterion, 1992); ET: Bernard G. Prusak, "Speech and Religion: The Word of God," in
Phenomenology and the "Theological Turn," which also includes Dominique Janicaud, *Le
tournant théologique de la phénoménologie français* (Paris: Éditions de l'Éclat, 1991), collected in *Phénoménologie de la vie*, vol. 4: *Sur l'éthique et la religion* (Paris: Presses
Universitaire de France, 2004), pp. 177-202; "Phénoménologie matérielle et langage (ou pathos et langage)," originally presented at Cerisy in 1996, and collected in *Phénoménologie
de la vie*, vol. 3, pp. 325-48; ET: "Material Phenomenology and Language (or Pathos and
Language)," trans. Leonard Lawlor, in *Continental Philosophy Review* 32 (1999): 343-65.

pearing constitutes the incontrovertible condition of every conceivable language . . . then the sense of a 'phenomenology of language' has been totally reversed."[28] "What is shown in this Word, what is made manifest, is life itself. . . . Language is the language of real life. It is in this sense that the logos can first be true, and in some way, always is true."[29] Henry's philosophy of language thus opposes systematically any view of language as autonomous, whose meaning might be deciphered independently, without any speaker, without any life in it. But in *Words of Christ*, Henry now envisions a different set of criteria through which this truth finds determination — or rather, only one criterion. What is important now is not merely life's phenomenal structure, so to speak, but more fundamentally the power to give life, since all of life's phenomenality consists first in this.

Words of Christ marks the culmination and fulfillment of this reversal. The premise of this book is not that the spoken words of Christ contain the answer to a philosophical question about the essence of language. Nor that a new philosophy of language is required to hear and understand the words of Christ. The premise is that an adequate philosophy of language founded on the phenomenality of life renders intelligible the unfathomable claim that Christ is the very Word of God, the Word of Life. Henry does not present an argument, nor an interpretation of a text in the classical sense, but a phenomenology of language that takes the words of Jesus as a guide for its reflection. This book does not merely repeat what Henry has carried out previously, not even on the question of language. As we will see, his own account of language is both placed in question here and reaffirmed in another register.

Henry's analysis of the words of Jesus proceeds by a series of distinctions that serve, step by step, to isolate a form of speech that is proper to Jesus alone. At one level, these distinctions first concern the referent of his speech, and on this level it is possible to distinguish what Jesus says about humanity and the human condition from what he says about him-

---

28. Michel Henry, "Phénoménologie matérielle et langage (ou pathos et langage)," in *Phénoménologie de la vie*, vol. 3, p. 344.

29. Michel Henry, *Phénoménologie matérielle* (Paris: Presses Universitaires de France, 1990), p. 131; ET: *Material Phenomenology*, trans. Scott Davidson (New York: Fordham University Press, 2008), p. 97.

self. But in considering the words he speaks about himself, we find that, at a deeper level, another and more important distinction is in play. This distinction does not consist in a difference of referent, with some words speaking of himself as man and others of himself as God, for example. It consists in a different mode of phenomenality, a distinct manner in which these words reveal what they say, the precise relationship between the saying and the said. On this basis, Henry then raises the question of how these words acquire legitimacy and are justified. And here another distinction arises, this time between the way they justify themselves and the way they find justification also in us.

Jesus' words first speak of them, his auditors, and equally of us insofar as we share in their human condition. Jesus draws our attention not only to what is important to us but also to what it is in us that determines us to be who we are, the principle of our thoughts and our actions. These words define the human essence as the heart and, to this extent, as fundamentally affective. Jesus tells us that we are children of God, of inestimable worth, and speaks of the necessities of life, of food, clothing, shelter, and the satisfaction of needs, in which human economic life consists. He also establishes an opposition between the invisible secret of the heart, seen by God, and the visibility of the world, the sole concern of the Pharisees, which he denounces. These words of Jesus constitute a wisdom and an ethic, available to anyone in principle. But other words of Jesus take a different tone. Far from building us up, they condemn us, and not merely our actions or our thoughts, but the evil that plagues us, the false images in which we think we see ourselves, idols of all sorts, our spontaneity, our narcissism. "Human nature is disqualified as a whole" (p. 20 below). A great difference arises between his words and us, and yet the truth of a painful affinity.

The radical character of what Jesus says about the human condition drives his listeners to wonder not only about the meaning of his words but also about who he is that speaks this way and by what right he does so. If he is capable of speaking with authority about the human condition, if he in fact knows that we are children of God, he must himself have intimate acquaintance with the process of divine generation, to the point of identifying with it. But far from speaking of himself, he instead demands an answer from the mouths of his listeners. Who do you say that I am? He poses the question first to his disciples, then to those who seek to ruin him. The Gospel narratives convey the encounters with the Pharisees as scenes of great importance, the site of a "more original conflict" (pp. 57-58) in which his authority is called into question; but these scenes culminate by calling into question their own pretend authority, leaving open the "very profound mystery" of his own.

For Henry, the Gospel of John develops the most profound source of legitimation with regard to the words of Christ. John is "not content with reproducing the confrontations which will lead to Jesus' condemnation and torment in all their tragic tension. His plan, at first glance unrealizable, is to validate Christ's affirmation of his status as Son by placing himself as it were at the interior of this affirmation and in being coextensive with its movement. More radically: by placing himself at the interior of the very position of being the Christ and in identifying with it" (p. 60). Grasping what he says now depends upon understanding the nature of this speech. The stakes are now higher, and the source of legitimation higher too, for if Christ is the Word of God, precisely his spoken Word, then the justification of this word "will only be able to come from God's word [*parole*] itself, lived in its original truth. It can only come from the Word [*Verbe*]" (p. 61). It is from that Word that the written words of John, and of the other Gospels, which remain human words in human language, borrow their authority and find their justification. The Law demands many witnesses, but Jesus links his own witness to his origin; "even if I testify on my own behalf, my testimony is valid because I know where I have come from" (p. 64).

The question now posed is whether another speech exists, other than the one that human beings customarily speak. Our language can be called the language of the world — first, because it refers to things in the world, to the domain of the visible in the broadest sense, both sensible and intelligible. Second, this language borrows its features from the phenomenality of the world, the way the world shows itself. Human words are other than what they speak of, indifferent to what they speak of, and powerless to create what they speak of, and that is why the ontological argument for the existence of God can be refuted by pointing to the difference between saying one has a $100 bill and actually having one. The predominant theories of language in modern and contemporary thought, starting with the theory of reference, presuppose this modality of appearing. But if the Christ is the Word of God, his words about himself cannot be understood on this premise.

For Henry, another philosophy of language is required, one that borrows its communicative power, not through reference to a common world, but from life. Life is a word in the sense that the language it speaks manifests what it communicates, not as something other than it, but as itself. Life communicates its suffering when and as it suffers, and the same goes for all of its affective tonalities, such as thirst and hunger, or sadness and joy. Philosophy does not need to look elsewhere for the evidence of such a language. *"The reality, of which the Word* [Verbe] *of Life speaks, is Life itself, of which it is the self-revelation, the actual reality"* (p. 88). The unique character of its speech is that it is what it tells us, and it is for this reason uncontestable. It is not an empty signification or theoretical affirmation capable of being filled with a content or of remaining empty. It is not capable of lying. In its speech we discover an "essential relationship particular to Christianity and which confers on it its extreme originality: *the relationship of Truth and Life"* (p. 75).

If the Christ *is* the Word of God, and not a prophet who only communicates this Word by speaking it, then the words of Christ about himself must also make accessible and intelligible the Word of God, wherever it appears. In this way, the legitimacy of his words find further confirmation when they clarify the other New Testament writings, the "timeless memorial" of his words, and the Jewish Scriptures, starting with Genesis and the creation of humanity by the Word of God. In giving life by speaking us, the Word of God says to us our own life. That is why we are destined to hear it, and why our nature is to understand it. If God is life, it follows that we know what God is because we are living, and yet none of us is capable of giving ourselves this condition. So if we are to understand how God gives life to us, we can do so only by knowing first how God offers life in himself. "Inasmuch as he is actually the Word [*Verbe*], *Christ is nothing other than the knowledge that God has of himself . . . the self-revelation of absolute Life"* (p. 88).

It remains to be shown where *in us* the legitimation of the Word of Christ can be found. How are we capable of hearing and understanding the Word of God, of knowing the one who speaks it in communicating himself? For Henry, the parables of Christ themselves contain an answer, and the parable of the sower above all, since it pertains directly to the question of hearing the Word of God. Here we learn that the Word of God forms the human heart in the very moment of hearing, to the point of constituting what is proper to each of us in the way we receive it.[30] Hearing may mean immediate refusal, and then the various forms of evil that diminish the heart take root in it, and in this sense determine it. Extreme difficulty may attend this hearing from the countless outrages that result from that evil, which suppress this hearing with a pain too heavy to bear.[31] Hearing, even in its own accomplishment, may lead to a kind of deafness, which the Johannine texts call the pride of life.[32] But life gives itself completely to every man and woman, to you and to me, making possible the very powers that define us, to act, to think, to will, to love in a freedom so concrete that it is ours, despite ourselves. We are powerless in the exercise of our own power to exercise it, so much so that we take ourselves as the foundation of our life and as its source. We thereby succumb to a major illusion about who we are by living, in all phenomenological truth, a lie — the self, the modern subject.

But the speech of life "completely subverts the place where we are given to ourselves in absolute Life" (p. 95). The question of its legitimacy gives way before the fullness of its content. Though incapable of giving life, human speech is not deaf to its sound, since we know with an invincible certainty the eloquence of life's speech, its suffering and its joy. It is silent, not because it does not make a sound, but because it cannot. Different by nature from the language we learn to speak as children, it makes this language possible. It is laden with meaning because it bears life and truth within it. All human speech depends upon it, since human life depends upon it.

In the hearing of these words, we find a strange restoration of humanity itself, in this strange but "decisive affinity" (p. 114) that makes hearing the words of Christ possible, since all human life in all of its

30. Cf. Psalm 32:15.
31. See also Michel Henry, "Théodicée dans la perspective d'une phénoménologie radicale," in *Phénoménologie de la vie*, vol. 4, pp. 81-94.
32. See 1 John 2:16: "For all that is in the world, the lust of the flesh and the lust of the eyes and the pride of life, is not of the Father but is of the world."

phenomenological integrity is spoken in them. Such an affinity is not achieved through any effort, but makes every effort possible. It does not merely qualify those that hear it, but also those that hate it, since this relation subsists even within those who, like Cain, wish to hide from its penetrating light. But in the end, perhaps the most striking character of the words of Christ is their omnipotent power, noted everywhere in the Gospels. Its omnipotence holds within it the power to give life again to men and women. And in the end, these words of Christ are also the prayer of a Son to his Father, that we may be one as they are one.

If the phenomenology of life attains the words of Christ to the point of revealing their true content, it does so only insofar as the Christ himself performs this work on his own. If the obstacle to achieving a philosophy of revelation consists in the impossibility in principle of philosophy ever succeeding in doing the work that revelation itself must do — namely, revealing itself, not with the resources of human knowledge, but on its own — then the final step in the reversal of phenomenology reaches a level of intelligibility without precedent in the history of philosophy. Christ tells us who we are.

Over the course of this book, the phenomenology of life is consumed in revelation. What begins as the painful affinity of a warranted condemnation ends in the joy of life's restoration, by one who has the power to give it. Hearing the word, in the end, means hearing one's very life said in it, so that it is we, in the end, who are the invincible proof of what it tells us. "My son, be attentive to my words; incline your ear to my sayings. Let them not escape from your sight; keep them within your heart. For they are life to him who finds them, and healing to all his flesh. Keep your heart with all vigilance; for from it flow the springs of life."[33] We find ourselves, and like the Samaritan woman we are compelled to ask, "Come, see a man who revealed everything to me . . . Could this be the Christ?"[34]

KARL HEFTY
The University of Chicago

33. Proverbs 4:20-22.
34. John 4:29.

Translator's Note

I have generally translated *vivant* as "living being" instead of just "living" (as *I Am the Truth* does), as that makes for a very awkward noun in English (especially in the singular). Yet, the reader should throughout be mindful of what Scott Davidson says in his translator's introduction to *Material Phenomenology:* "With respect to the latter term ["living beings"], one should bear in mind that Henry seeks to distinguish 'the living' from 'beings' in the sense of external objects, and so the emphasis should remain on the fact that 'living beings' are alive and not that they are beings" (xvi).

I have not adopted the common translation of *pathétique* as "pathetic" (or *"pathetik"*) which, despite all caution on the part of respective translators, simply ends up sounding quite pathetic. (Anyone who has ever listened to Beethoven's *Pathétique*[1] or Tchaikovsky's *Symphony Pathétique*[2] will know that there is simply no way *pathétique* can mean or be transliterated as "pathetic.") Susan Emanuel says in her brief foreword to the English translation of *I Am the Truth* that "Michel Henry uses French *pathos* and *pathétique* in what amounts to the sense of these words' Greek roots. For *pathos,* that semantic domain extends from 'anything that befalls one' through 'what one has suffered, one's experience' (including its negative inflection in something like English 'suffering'), to 'any passive state or condition.' The adjectival form . . . means 'subject to

---

1. Piano Sonata no. 8 in C minor, op. 13.
2. Symphony No. 6, op. 74.

feeling, capable of feeling something.'"[3] To avoid "pathetic" I have instead employed the noun "pathos" or used "pathos-filled."

Most centrally for the argument in this book, I have translated both *parole/Parole* and *Verbe* as "word." After exploring several unsatisfactory possibilities for distinguishing the two in English, I decided to stick with the same term (as to a large extent Henry's argument is their final identification with each other anyway). Whenever he uses the term *Verbe* I have provided the French in parenthesis and occasionally I have done so for *Parole* as well, especially when it is capitalized and occurs in the same sentence with *Verbe* (which happens fairly frequently). *Parole* is the more active term in French and refers to the act of speaking. "Speech" is its primary translation, but in most contexts that simply does not fit here. *Verbe* is the more static noun and designates the word as such. French also has the term *mot,* which Henry does employ at times, often to refer to words as "terms" for something else. When *mot* had to be translated as "word" I have also indicated the French. Henry's argument is mostly about the *paroles* of Christ, namely the words he speaks, but he shows how Christ himself is God's *Parole,* i.e., God's Word, God's speaking to humans. Therefore, according to Henry's argument, Christ is also rightly the incarnate Word [*Verbe*] of God, namely the Logos/Word of the prologue to the Gospel of John ("In the beginning was the *word,*" which is translated as *verbe* in French). Since Henry also criticizes the "logos" of the Greek philosophers, which becomes an abstract reason without materiality, "logos" would not be an appropriate "translation" of *Verbe* in this context.

Wherever I have provided a note or comment not in the original text I have used square brackets. Wherever the phrase "emphasis mine" appears, apart from this Translator's Introduction, it owes to Henry himself (as do, obviously, the italics themselves). Henry typically provides biblical references for the biblical passages he cites; these appear in parentheses following citations. Occasionally I have supplied such references where they were missing in the original: in such cases, the reference appears within square brackets. In instances where a particular biblical reference is incomplete (e.g., where Henry has quoted three verses but cited only two), I have silently corrected. All biblical references, unless other-

---

3. *I Am the Truth,* "Note on Terminology," n.p.

wise noted, are to the New Revised Standard Version (NRSV), published in 1989 by the National Council of Churches in the USA. With respect to internal (and not always consistent) capitalization of terms such as Word or Revelation, or such phrases as Word of Life, I have generally followed Henry's own choices with two exceptions (at the copyeditor's suggestion): "sons" of God (with reference to humanity) is lower-cased (Henry is inconsistent in this regard); capitals are retained only for "the Son of God" with reference to Christ. Likewise, "father," when referencing human fatherhood, is lower-cased; only with reference to God does "Father" retain a capital (principally in the middle section of chapter three).

Finally a comment on gender. Like most French philosophical writing, Henry's reference to humans (or, for that matter, the divine) is almost entirely male. God is always Father, humans are always sons. All pronouns are exclusively male. I have aimed in this translation for more inclusive language and have therefore often translated references to humans as plural when they are singular ("man") in French. As Henry is making an argument about the human condition in general and takes care (especially in this book) to distinguish *all* humans as "sons" from the one "Arch-Son" (Christ), the move to the plural did not seem to distort his argument. He does actually claim late in *I Am the Truth* (and once, more weakly, in *Words of Christ*) that his argument refers just as much to women as to men: "This essential common truth is nothing other and nothing less than what inhabits each determination of virility and femininity, to wit, *the fact that this determination is given to itself and that this givenness to itself takes place in the same way, is the same, for man as for woman.* It is, for each 'human being' — man or woman — the condition of Son: the living person given to himself in the self-giving of absolute Life. It is this self-givenness that is Identical in each: Christ, God. Neither male nor female: Son of God" (*I Am the Truth,* 251).[4] While that may not alleviate the problems of his own heavy use of male language, it does seem to render permission for being more inclusive in translation.

---

4. Emphasis his. For the context of the argument see *I Am the Truth,* pp. 248-51. In *Words of Christ,* he once speaks explicitly of men and women, but merely mentions both genders in the sentence without elaborating any further.

WORDS OF CHRIST

Introduction

According to Christian theology (we will wonder later about its plausibility or legitimacy from a philosophical point of view) Christ's nature is twofold, at the same time both human and divine. Insofar as Christ is the Incarnation of the Word [*Verbe*] of God, it is this Word and thus God as such who lives in Christ. Yet because the flesh in which the Word [*Verbe*] became incarnate is similar to our flesh, Christ is also a human being like us. In taking on our condition he also simultaneously assumed its finitude. This finitude is precisely that of the flesh. It can be recognized by multiple signs. The most distinctive is an array of needs indicating that no flesh is self-sufficient. It constantly requires that we nourish it, take care of it, and protect it in various ways, both from perils that menace it from the outside and from unceasing internal danger — that is, that we attend to all the needs that urgently require to be satisfied. Each flesh is thus compelled to sustain the life that is in it and which clamors without respite for the conditions of survival.

In actuality, it is this life that is finite. It is as incapable of giving itself life as it is of maintaining it by its own means. That is why this finite living flesh presents two sets of correlative natures. On the one hand, the impressions which constitute it are negative emotional tonalities, those of the discomfort of need, dissatisfaction, desire, the multiple forms and nuances of pain and suffering by which it is besieged. In all these tonalities, their tiresome and disagreeable content expresses the fundamental *lack* that affects the flesh inasmuch as it is incapable of being self-sufficient. Yet this first set of traits results in a second feature proper to

3

each flesh, its dynamism. Precisely because none of the needs that mark our fleshly condition can remain without response, because they emerge with an insistence whose pressure quickly becomes intolerable, various impulses arise in our flesh itself. By these the flesh endeavors to change its discomfort into the well-being of a provisionally gratified desire. In this way the grip that the system of our needs exerts on us corresponds to the set of activities necessary for their satisfaction. What one calls "the economy" takes its motivation from our incarnate condition, whatever its deviancies and perversions or the reversals to which it will be subject throughout history. As Marx says (who refers to labor throughout his oeuvre as a "subjective, individual, and living" work), if work were to break off for even a single day, humanity would vanish.

Like each one of us, Christ lived this finitude of the incarnate condition with its limitations and its rhythms which give emphasis to daily existence and confer on it its particular temporality. He worked for a long period of his life. And when, during his public life and in order to dedicate himself entirely to his mission, he gave to his disciples and to those who welcomed him the tasks that one improperly calls material (although they are composed of entirely subjective impressions and motivations), he continued to experience hunger, thirst, fatigue, sadness, and tears before suffering the torments and insults of his Passion.

If Christ's nature is twofold, one can imagine that his speaking [*parole*] is also dual. Not that it would be marked by duplicity, in the way human speech is subject to worldly schemes or practiced in pretence and falsehoods. Christ's speaking is dual in a completely different sense, that is as precise as it is radical: *sometimes a human word* [parole] *is at stake in it and sometimes that of God.* Must not an analysis of Christ's words henceforth be obligated to ask in regard to each of them: who speaks? Is it the human Jesus, who has no pillow on which to lay his head and who asks for a drink from a Samaritan woman? Or is it instead the Word [*Verbe*] of God himself, who is the Word [*Parole*] of an eternal God and who says in his own words [*paroles*]: "Heaven and earth will pass away, but my words will not pass away" (Luke 21:33)?

This essential distinction between a human and a divine word must be subjected to rigorous examination. Is it not advisable to distinguish in each word the manner in which it speaks? On the one hand, one should

4

consider the word in itself as a speaking word, in its saying and in its manner of saying; on the other hand, one must consider what it speaks as well as what it says, its content.[1]

The nature of human language in general must be elucidated in regard to human speech. During the twentieth century its analysis has become one of the major topics of reflection. It has given rise to numerous complementary and conflicting theories, which are nevertheless grouped together into a far-reaching "philosophy of language" whose varied presuppositions, whether they be phenomenological, analytical, or psychoanalytical, have not managed to shatter a final unity. This unity consists precisely in regarding language in its act of speech as different from that about which it speaks, its "content." Thus it is easy to separate in each human word the nature of the language that it brings into play from the objects it designates and describes. Is not language considered in itself identical, whether I say, like Spinoza, "the dog barks" or "the concept of the dog does not bark"? One must give an account for the reason why this separation between the saying of language and what it says arises in all human speaking.

Yet one must make an even more important remark. Do not the varied conceptions of language present a second common trait, one that is purely negative? They all concern human language. Insofar as Christ is speaking to humans, he uses their own language; thus the way in which he speaks to them manifests the properties of human language. These very properties are studied by the analyses of language I have mentioned.

If we now assume that the Word [*Verbe*] of God speaks a completely different language, different in principle from human language, we are compelled to recognize that his Word [*Parole*] eludes all the conceptions of language which I have just mentioned. Because it is unilaterally directed at human language, philosophy of language would reveal a gaping deficiency: it knows nothing about the word which alone matters when all is said and done — the Word [*Parole*] of God, that is to say, *the way in which God speaks to us.* Moreover, this would not only be a simple deficiency, but a disastrous and definitive eclipse. Not only would the Word

---

1. [Henry is here employing terminology from contemporary philosophy of language. See the following paragraph. — Trans.]

5

[*Parole*] of God remain misunderstood; we would have lost any conception of it.

Christ's words, or at any rate a number of them, have come down to us. They are contained in the "Logia," collections whose origins are beyond doubt. The apocryphal gospel attributed to Thomas, rediscovered in Egypt in a Gnostic library, consists of a simple enumeration of Jesus' words. Collections of this sort have circulated since earliest times. Nothing prevents us from assuming that some of the assertions they recount were written down in Christ's lifetime, by listeners, by disciples, or even by an appointed secretary. Even if the gospel attributed to Thomas was composed in the middle of the second century, it still provides proof of the great age of the Logia, as several of their utterances are found in the Gospels according to Matthew, Mark, and Luke.[2] The evangelists have obviously drawn from it (without, for all that, underestimating the decisive importance of the apostles' oral preaching) so as to construct a teaching intended to transmit the divine Revelation contained in Christ's words.

Yet we must be in a position to understand these words. One might wonder why that would not be the case, since these words are precisely formulated in our language? Nevertheless a good many people do not understand them. As Christ himself said, citing Isaiah, but in regard to his own teaching: "They have ears and they do not hear" (see, below, chapter 9). If one wants to reduce the depth of this deafness a bit, one might say that they grasp only the human sense of these words, reducing them to respectable or even admirable moral precepts, but without proof that they would be anything but the sayings of someone inspired, a wise man or a prophet. It remains to be established that at stake is the word [*parole*] of God or (if one prefers) that Christ who spoke them is his Word [*Verbe*]. It is precisely this that many did not believe and continue not to believe.

Contrary to the falsehoods of the positivistic, pseudo-historical, and atheistic exegesis of the nineteenth century, it can therefore be assumed that Christ's words are in no way invented by late Christian communi-

---

2. On this one should refer to the admirable work of Henri-Charles Puech, *En quête de la gnose*, vol. II, *Sur l'Évangile de Thomas* (Paris: Gallimard, 1978).

ties. They present themselves to us as authentic documents. Yet nothing prevents us from regarding them as human words, in all senses of that term. They are words pronounced by a human being speaking to other humans in human language and speaking to them about themselves. About themselves, that is to say, about their nature, their qualities, their defects, telling them what they should do, where good and evil are: really, an ethics.

Nonetheless, not all the words Christ speaks to humans concern them. Some tell them not about themselves but about what he is, he who is speaking to them. And these are the most stunning ones. They form what one must call *a discourse by Christ about himself.* And this remarkable discourse contains the most important part of his teaching, the part from which all the rest follows — statements that inescapably, upon reflection, are without equal in the history of human thought. These words spoken to humans in their own language, and in which Christ speaks to them about himself, never actually speak of him as if he were one among them, as if he were a human being. In a veiled fashion, at first indirectly and then openly, he refers to himself as really the Son of God and hence in the eyes of those who were there, as God himself. And one sees that these astounding assertions are not merely the products of late fables of fanatic communities, insomuch as they were the direct cause of his condemnation and his death. The Jews were used to simple prophets and endured them as well as could be expected. John the Baptist was not beheaded because he prophesied or baptized, but, as is well-known, because of the cunning of a woman whose adultery he had denounced.

Now, if in speaking about himself Christ refers to himself as the Son of God, of "his Father," as of the same nature with him, speaking in his name and saying what his Father told him, what his Father says, then the question to which we have alluded from the outset retains its full force. Due to his twofold nature, does Christ not speak to us in two different ways, sometimes in human speech, sometimes as the Word itself of God? Consequently, is not a crucial analysis of these two forms of speech essential, despite the difficulty they raise? It is easy for us today to speak about human language, its nature, its capacity of establishing communication between humans, and this because of the rapid development of contemporary philosophy of language. The possibility of analyzing the

Word of God in the same way nevertheless appears beyond our reach. What components do we have at our disposal? Would one not have to know what God is in order to know *the way in which he speaks to us and in order to understand it?* Or rather: How could a language which would be that of God really be understood in our own language? Without doubt, we would be able to grasp what he allows us to capture in this supposed language of God, if it were to adopt the structure of a human language. Most certainly we understand quite a few (and quite impressive) things in the words of Christ written in the Logia and transmitted by the Gospels. Yet is not the ultimate question to learn *whether this Word is of divine origin and essence, and thus to know with an unassailable conviction that it really is that of God* — and no one else's?

For centuries the Word of God was immediately lived as such, as his Word. This situation has progressively deteriorated in modern times. Not only because the teaching of this word — indispensable for its transmission from one generation to the other — was prohibited by establishments of public teaching and by education in general, banned in the merciless combat against Christianity by the totalitarian dogmatism of so-called "democratic" nations. In fact it is the organization of the entire world with its omnipresent materialism, its sordid ideas of social success, of money, of power, of instant pleasure, its exhibitionism and its voyeurism, all kinds of depravity, its worship of new idols, of subhuman machines, of all that is less than human, the reduction of humans to biology and, through that, to lifeless matter — it is all this (of which education has become the alternately scandalous, blind, or absurd reflection), this unceasing commotion of actuality with its sensational events and its ludicrous shows, which perpetually masks the silence where the word speaks that we no longer hear.

That being said, our concern here does not focus on the historical phenomenon of modernity which is constantly on the verge of collapse into its own nothingness. The question that must be asked is a question of principle. Is it possible for humans to hear in their own language a word [*parole*] which would speak in another language, namely that of God or more exactly of his Word [*Verbe*]? And if not, how could one at least ensure the existence of such a word? I strive to respond to a question that involves human destiny in a very concrete fashion. To this end, I will take Christ's words themselves as guide for my reflections. For without a doubt they contain the response. In the same way, in fact, as any scientific assertion, and at bottom any human affirmation, carries within itself *a claim to truth,* so Christ's word is distinguished by a claim, inordinate in the eyes and ears of many of his contemporaries. His claim is not only to transmit a divine revelation but purely and simply to be in himself this Revelation, the Word [*Parole*] of God. By following the sequence of his words step by step I will endeavor to see whether they are capable of justifying such an assurance: speaking the Word of this God whom Christ himself claims to be.

In this examination, I will naturally observe neither a chronological nor a pre-arranged order. It will also not be an order of foundation, beginning with propositions — axioms, presuppositions, or principles — on which all the others rest, an order of which I also know nothing, at least at the moment. Drawing my inspiration from the great distinctions briefly outlined in this introduction, I will study successively:

1. The words of Christ considered as a human being, speaking to humans in their own language and speaking to them about themselves.

2. The words of Christ considered as a human being, speaking to humans in their own language, but speaking no longer about them but about himself.

Inasmuch as in speaking about himself Christ portrays himself as the Messiah, saying to humans what his Father has said to him, and in this way presenting himself as the Word [*Verbe*] of God, one must also examine:

3. In what manner the word [*parole*] of Christ considered as that of the Word [*Verbe*], as the Word [*Parole*] of God, differs from human speaking [*parole*] in general. How does it speak and what does it say? What are its essential characteristics?

4. Finally, how are humans capable of hearing and of understanding this Word which is not theirs but that of God?

Whatever the twists and turns entailed by the order of my examination, it is only by producing the analyses it requires that I will be in a position to provide a response to these questions. In the final account, a correct understanding of our human condition rests on this response. This understanding will be completely different, depending on whether it arises from a specific definition which confines it in a circle (an imprisonment particular to any form of humanism) or whether, capable of hearing the Word of God and open to listening, the human being is shown to be intelligible in its interior relation to this absolute Truth and Love one calls God.

CHAPTER I

Words That Christ, as a Human Being, Addresses to Humans in Their Own Language — about Themselves

One can highlight in the Gospels a certain number of remarks which could be those of a human being, namely of the man Jesus. These words would be distinctive only by the depth of their views and by the conclusions which one draws from them in order to provide rules of conduct for their listeners. This type of speech constitutes what one might call a wisdom speech. Moreover, often such remarks do not isolate individuals, but consider them instead in their environment, indeed in their relation with the whole universe. The judgment concerns the human being; the advice resulting from it consequently implies a judgment on the universe itself.

This is the case for two singular passages, one from Mark, the other from Matthew. Furthermore, their importance is due to the way in which they tackle the problem of evil in a decisive fashion: evil is not in the universe, but is found solely in the human being. This thesis is laid out in regard to a question that is both very specific and very practical, if not to say trivial. "Then the disciples approached and said to him, 'Do you know that the Pharisees took offense when they heard what you said?'" [Matt. 15:12]. Once again opposing the ritualistic formalism of Jewish religion, Jesus simply declared that it is not necessary to wash one's hands before eating. Yet this declaration, provocative for all the legalists, makes a metaphysical affirmation. It is not content only with stating, as Hegel will nineteen centuries later, that "only the stone is innocent." Rather, it extends this assertion to everything that is similar to the stone. Any material process, all that is studied by science, everything that does not sense or experience anything, everything that is different from humans, is all innocent. That is why "he [Jesus] declared all foods clean" [Mark 7:19].

Instead, it is in the heart — where humans experience everything else and also experience themselves — where one is human in distinction from all the "things." The heart contains evil; evil comes forth from it. Thus Matthew: "Do you not see that whatever goes into the mouth enters the stomach, and goes out into the sewer? But what comes out of the mouth proceeds from the heart, and this is what defiles. For out of the heart come evil intentions, murder, adultery, fornication, theft, false witness, slander. These are what defile a person, but to eat with unwashed hands does not defile" (Matt. 15:11-20). One finds a similar text in Mark (7:14-23): "There is nothing outside a person that by going in can defile, but the things that come out are what defile. . . . For it is from within, from the human heart, that evil intentions come. . . . All these evil things come from within, and they defile a person."

The demarcation of the place of evil, here called defilement, concerns not only an ethics; it implies a general definition of the human condition which, as we have just said, uses the "heart" as its principle. The identification of human reality with the "heart" has an unprecedented significance. It testifies that in distinction from the things of the universe which do not sense and do not experience anything — and which for this reason would be unable to be either good or evil — humans are those who experience themselves. It is for this exact reason that humans find themselves at the same time capable of experiencing and sensing all that surrounds them, namely the world and the things which show themselves within it. Yet experiencing oneself constitutes the distinctive feature of life. Living is in fact nothing else: suffering what one is and rejoicing in it, rejoicing in oneself. The "heart" — this term which recurs so often in the Gospels — hence designates human reality as essentially emotive, which is what it really is. Affectivity is the essence of life. Furthermore, in the transmitted collection of words, Christ employs the term "life" in order to refer to human reality, our reality, *our life.* The most concrete Synoptic texts say the same thing as the Johannine texts or Paul's letters.

From the philosophical point of view, the definition of humans as

12

deriving their reality from the Affectivity of life, and thus as living beings who do not cease to experience themselves in suffering or in joy, has revolutionary import. On the historical level, it shatters the horizon of Greek thought which defined the human as a rational being: humans are distinguished from animals precisely through Reason, as being "endowed with Logos." The Christian definition, which turns the human being into a "living being" [*un vivant*], nevertheless has nothing to do with its current biological interpretation. According to the biological interpretation, what one traditionally calls "life" is actually reduced to a set of material processes consistent with those studied by physics. The scientific view is focused on this realm, which Matthew's and Mark's description marks as the "outside" — where there is no evil because there is really nothing human.

This establishes a distinction between, on the one hand, what as outside of humans is foreign to them and, on the other hand, the "heart" where humans experience themselves and all the particulars of experience — their affections, their desires, and, for example, "the evil intentions: fornication, theft, murder, adultery, avarice, wickedness, deceit, licentiousness, envy, slander, pride, folly" (Mark's version). Such a distinction, as important as it may be, in no way permits us to elevate ourselves above the human order: quite to the contrary, it serves to define it. At stake is an order which is no longer that of things but of the life which experiences itself in its sufferings, its evil cravings, or its immense joy of living.

In this way one sees a movement of thought constantly occurring in the Gospels, which accompanies us from one order of reality to another. The at times extraordinary circumstances in which such a displacement takes place do not suffice to mask their evidence. After a night of fruitless fishing, Simon and his colleagues upon Christ's command throw their nets once again into the waters of the lake of Gennesaret. When their nets are ripping under the weight of the fish, they are so terrified that Simon asks the Lord to go away. We are familiar with Christ's response: "Do not be afraid; from now on you will be catching people" (Luke 5:1-11).

The apparently very simple distinction operating between "things" and "humans" can nevertheless only be understood in the context of the thought of the Gospels. The people in question are living and incarnate beings, inasmuch as we have been led to recognize from our first reflection on the person of Christ defined by the Incarnation of the Word.[1] Incarnate beings are not beings that have a body similar to things — an objective material body incapable of sensing anything. Incarnate beings are beings that have flesh, indeed, who are flesh: this moving and unbreakable totality of sensible, affective, and dynamic intuitions, which constitutes the concrete reality of the fleshly beings we are. These beings feel hunger, thirst, cold, the discomfort of unsatisfied need, the pain of effort, fear of obstacle, resentment against anything opposed to or greater than them, contempt for anything inferior to them or considered to be such.

That is to say that the world with which these incarnate beings have to deal is no longer one which confronts pure minds or a rational subject — the abstract world of theoretical knowing and of science with its objects which are themselves abstract, bare of all sensible quality, defined by mathematical parameters. The world of incarnate beings is composed of sensible objects, carved up and determined by needs and affects, carriers of all the values that life confers on them. In this way, the human world is the world of living beings, a life-world — *Lebenswelt,* as the German philosophers call it. The opposition that Christianity establishes between the human being and the world is in no way a theoretical distinction between a subject of knowledge and its object. It separates incarnate beings from this life-world which is theirs, a world of values corresponding to needs, to drives, and to emotions which form the substance of our flesh. This opposition constantly affirms the primacy of the human, understood as the fleshly living Self, over the whole of things useful to his or her life and which gain from it their value.

When speaking to humans about themselves, Christ also continuously places before their gaze their superiority over the entire universe. This superiority motivates one of the major criticisms that one meets in a good many Gospel passages, especially in this text from Matthew (6:25-34): "Therefore I tell you, do not worry about your life, what you will eat

---

1. [Henry is referring to his previous book *Incarnation: Une phenomenologie de la chair* (*Incarnation: A Phenomenology of the Flesh*), where he examined this question in detail. A translation of this work is in preparation. — Trans.]

or what you will drink, or about your body, what you will wear. Is not life more than food, and the body more than clothing? Look at the birds of the air; they neither sow nor reap nor gather into barns, and yet your heavenly Father feeds them. Are you not of more value than they? . . . . Consider the lilies of the field, how they grow; they neither toil nor spin, yet I tell you, even Solomon in all his glory was not clothed like one of these. . . . So do not worry about tomorrow, for tomorrow will bring worries of its own."

The point of impact of this celebrated criticism is difficult to delimit. For in contrasting humans with the world they put into play, the criticism concerns a world that is less than the human. Yet it immediately turns around against humans themselves inasmuch as they put their interest in this world which is less than them. Making what is inferior to them the source of their lust, creating a network of pseudo-values which henceforth regulate their desires and conduct, they devalue themselves at the same time. Humans' concealment of their own condition and of anything eminent it contains, corresponds to the overestimation of the world and its objects that have become its ideals or its idols. Hence Christ's strange and categorical declaration: "Are you not worth more than these?"

Henceforth, the relation between our own life and this world where we develop our projects and concern ourselves with their realization must be deepened if we want to understand the reversal of the hierarchy that we establish spontaneously between them. We are preoccupied with one, the things of the world, but forget the second — this life which is ours and which is infinitely more valuable than all the rest. The passage from Matthew that immediately precedes the one on which we have just commented, responds to our question. Behind the ethical character of formulated precepts, one should recognize the unfathomable significance of this response. *The relation between the world and our life is here proposed under the form of a radical opposition between the visible and the invisible.* The world is the reign of the visible, life that of the invisible. To the world belongs everything susceptible to appearing before a gaze, presenting itself as a spectacle in a "light" which is the world itself. This light comes from placing things at a distance or within a "horizon" of exteriority on the screen on which all things appear for us — in this "outside," this "in front of," this "before us," this "before humans" which is the world as such.[2] The Gospels often call the light of this horizon of visibility "the glory of the world," in contrast to the invisible revelation of the life in us, referred to as "the secret" (a secret that consequently we are ourselves), or also as "the glory of God."

Yet this radical division between the two realms of the visible and of the invisible concerns us, who belong to the world as much as to life. On the one hand, the human being shows itself in the world as an objective body similar to that of things. In this way it gives itself to be seen by other humans as well as by itself. When this body acts, its action assumes the appearance of an external displacement; it appears objectively as this body. Yet we know that the body is only the visible appearance of a living flesh, experiencing itself in life and invisible as such. Only this living flesh, composed of our impressions, of our desires, of our efforts to satisfy them — thus of our sorrows and our joys — constitutes our true reality, the heart and the secret of our being. Because this invisible flesh defines our true corporeality, all our actions considered in their effective reality are also accomplished in it. Of this reality one always grasps only an outside appearance which envelops it, so to speak. The possibility of the hypocrisy that inhabits the human world is born in this gap between our real actions and their appearance. We see here that this hypocrisy is in no way limited to words but has as much to do with actions.

We are therefore now in a position to understand the text in Matthew (6:1-18): "Beware of practicing your piety before others in order to be seen by them. . . . So whenever you give alms, do not sound a trumpet before you, as the hypocrites do in the synagogues and in the streets, so that they may be praised by others. . . . But when you give alms, do not let your left hand know what your right hand is doing, so that your alms may be done in secret. . . . And whenever you pray, do not be like the hypocrites; for they love to stand and pray in the synagogues and at the

---

2. [Most of the terminology Henry employs here refers to phenomenology, especially as outlined by Edmund Husserl. Phenomenology studies the phenomena which appear to consciousness. For Husserl all such phenomena appear within a horizon, or context, which makes it possible to perceive and to study such appearances. The terminology of the "life-world" which Henry used in the previous paragraph is also Husserl's. Henry both assumes and is critical of Husserl's phenomenology in his treatment. — Trans.]

street corners, so that they may be seen by others. . . . But whenever you pray, go into your room and shut the door. . . . And whenever you fast, do not look dismal, like the hypocrites, for they disfigure their faces so as to show others that they are fasting. . . . But when you fast, put oil on your head and wash your face, so that your fasting may not be seen by others."

Beyond its obvious ethical meaning, this criticism of the attitude that one notices most often among human beings and which consists in seeking in the gaze of others a justification for what one does and thus of what one is oneself — one's own "prestige" — rests on the crucial conflict between the visible and the invisible, the external and the internal, a theme of opposition that runs through Christ's entire teaching. A similar opposition grounds the very *possibility* of hypocrisy, namely that between the reality held in the "heart" and the appearance of the world. It is also at work in the polemic against the Pharisees whose deceit is not their least flaw. It is encountered again in this passionate diatribe by Christ: "Woe to you, scribes and Pharisees, hypocrites! For you are like whitewashed tombs, which on the outside look beautiful, but inside they are full of the bones of the dead and of all kinds of filth. So you also on the outside look righteous to others, but inside you are full of hypocrisy and lawlessness" (Matt. 23:27-28).

The opposition of the visible to the invisible, which is taken up again and formulated explicitly in the Christian creed, has decisive philosophical import. It does not trace a line of division between what is human and what is divine, the invisible referring to "Heaven" and becoming like the latter a sort of "netherworld" or of mythical "beyond," an object of skepticism for those who claim to confine themselves to what one can see and touch. Rather, the invisible concerns the human being itself and his or her true reality. A human being is really twofold, visible and invisible at the same time. The analysis of the body has established that the body is given to us in two different fashions: on the one hand, under the form of an external, visible body in the fashion of other bodies in the universe; on the other hand, each person lives inwardly in his or her own body under the form of the invisible flesh, suffering and desiring, and is at one with it.

Even so, these two terms we have learned to distinguish are in no way situated on the same plane. Reduced to its objective aspect, our body is only one representation among others, a sort of reflection like that seen in a mirror. It also has the lightness, the transparency, the lack of reality, and the powerlessness of this image. This represented body, the object offered to the gaze, draws its reality, its stunning, dynamic, and pathos-filled [*pathétique*] depth which makes of our incarnate condition what it is, from our invisible flesh. It is hence advisable to affirm this at first glance perplexing truth: as far as human beings are concerned, it is in our invisible subjectivity where our actual reality is found. Our outside appearance is precisely only a semblance. This unusual thesis results from Christ's polemic against the Pharisees' hypocrisy, as well as from his analysis of evil. Whether it is a matter of fasting, of prayer, of good or evil action, these various activities escape the visible world and are accomplished where they remain unknown to others: in secret.

A first glance at a rather limited number of Christ's words aimed at humans has sufficed to unveil intuitions of such depth that Western thought of Greek inspiration will have a hard time assimilating them. One will have to await the beginning of the nineteenth century until Maine de Biran, a philosopher of genius, would make the discovery of a subjective body [that is] opposed to the object-body of the tradition. Is it not remarkable that the conception of action as an operation of this subjective body — having its location in our flesh and hence as invisible as this flesh is (a conception which is supported by the brief passages of Christ's teaching to which we have alluded) — remains misunderstood today?

Nevertheless, as profound as Christ's words concerning the human condition are — the definition of this condition as living flesh in its opposition to the objective body of the world, the decisive distinction of the visible and the invisible as condition of this opposition, the entirely original conception of action which equally results from this — as true as they must appear today to any individual capable of authentic reflection on him- or herself and on the world in which he or she lives, they are still human words. Very great thinkers, such as Descartes or Maine de Biran, or even to a lesser degree Schopenhauer, have been able to recover the founding intuitions. They are human words in all respects, since he who uttered them is a human being, speaking to humans in their own language, so that they would be able to understand. Furthermore, these words speak to them about their own existence in this world where it takes place and finally of the course of action which they ought to follow in such a world. The body of these speeches — their content, their presuppositions, and their approach — determine what one could call a "human system," where everything proceeds from humans and all is referred to them. One could also call it a "humanism" or, as we have already observed, a wisdom speech. The origin, the nature, and the purpose of this system explain its coherence, since it is always the same reality that is in question. This is why all the great civilizations, before even being civilizations of the written word, have produced insights of this sort, permitting humans to live and to survive in following the prescriptions engraved on them as the constituents of their nature.

Many other words of Christ are inscribed, it seems, into such a system where everything concerns the human being. In particular this is the case for the very harsh remarks by which Christ refuses the subordination of the human being to a network of laws to which one would have to conform one's action. The reversal of a hierarchy which places the law above humans is all the more impressive as the law in question is the religious law. This appears most radically during the open conflict with the Pharisees. "Is it lawful to cure people on the sabbath, or not?" Since it is life that is at stake in healing, the object of the reversal is discovered in all clarity: what is more than the Law is precisely life. Yet this subordination of the Law to life is at work not only in the exceptional case of an illness; it is valid everywhere in daily existence. "If one of you has a child or an ox that has fallen into a well, will you not immediately pull it out on a sabbath day?" That the ideal prescriptions of the Law lose all credence, faced with this sudden naked appearance of life in its most banal forms, is an affirmation so much more revealing and disagreeable as it is addressed to those who are in charge of it, "the lawyers and Pharisees": "and they could not reply to this" (Luke 14:3-6).

Another passage in Luke, cited less often, seems to push this appeal to humans to the extreme, so that they would find and recognize in themselves the principle of their decisions and of their acts. It evokes the surprising moment when Christ asks that people set themselves up as judges of conflicts that may come between them and others instead of resorting to external bodies such as courts: "And why do you not judge for yourselves what is right? Thus, when you go with your accuser before a magistrate, on the way make an effort to settle the case" (Luke 12:57-58). We know how Paul, who quite obviously knew these teachings, will impart a decisive significance to them. But the theme is present everywhere in the Synoptic Gospels: "The sabbath was made for humankind and not humankind for the sabbath" (Mark 2:27).

The one who manages to bring to closure in himself what we call for this reason a human system, namely he who has just traced its broad outlines, has himself all the appearances of a human being. Other than the strange expression "the Son of Man" which recurs ceaselessly in the Gospels (but which means exactly the opposite of what it may seem to say at first glance), one can also cite many passages where, not only content to behave as a human, Christ explicitly refers to himself as one. "A scribe then approached and said, 'Teacher, I will follow you wherever you go.' And Jesus said to him, 'Foxes have holes, and birds of the air have nests; but the Son of Man has nowhere to lay his head'" (Matt. 8:19-20; also Luke 9:57-58). With the exception of sin, which according to theology Christ does not have, has Christ not assumed human nature all the way to the end, all the way to death? Will not the first generation of Fathers affirm this human nature of Christ constantly against heresy: "he felt hunger, so that we would comprehend that his humanity was true and indisputable"?[3]

According to this same theology, however, he who has assumed our human nature fully is also the Word [*Verbe*] of God. Assuming human nature [for the Word] does not mean to be annihilated in it, but rather *to live in it as the Word* [*Verbe*]. He is the Christ precisely because this Word [*Verbe*] remains in the human Jesus. The problem is knowing whether this presence of the Word [*Verbe*] of God in Christ is only an article of faith or whether, to the contrary, *it is itself revealed in its own truth* — a problem that we will leave aside provisionally. Christ, considered as a human being, speaks to humans, using their own language in order to speak to them about themselves. Let us be content for the moment to observe how in these words one sees this supposed human system, which would turn Christianity into a sort of wise insight or even one form of "spirituality" among others, first crack and then disintegrate entirely.

3. Irenaeus, *Against Heresies* (Paris: Cerf, 1991), 631.

CHAPTER 2

Disintegration of the Human World as a Result of Christ's Words

The words that Christ speaks to humans have brought to light the singularity they attach to the human condition. Do they not challenge the notion that humans habitually form about themselves, when they consider themselves beings of the world — and this in a twofold sense? On the one hand, they think of themselves as beings who appear in this world, their body precisely serving as the fashion in which they show themselves as such, to others as well as to themselves. Yet they also relate to things in the universe via their bodies in a manner which is first of all practical, not theoretical. What humans actually demand from things, from these multiple and qualitatively differentiated objects by which they are surrounded, is the satisfaction of their needs. This is how what we have called a human system takes shape. We now see more clearly that it designates the set of concrete relations that beings form among themselves and with the world in regard to the conservation and the development of their life. The extraordinary depth of Christianity has been to make us comprehend that the world is only the outside appearance of this twofold network of relations whose reality hangs together in the invisible of our life — precisely in our flesh, of which the body itself is only the external and visible aspect.

Yet we have equally seen, if only in allusive fashion, that philosophical thought is capable of elevating itself to these intuitions which introduce us to a new conception of the human. A type of wisdom is linked to this which still is the concern of humanism. Even in Christ's teachings, are not propositions like "each day has its own sorrow," "no human can serve two masters," "any kingdom divided against itself must perish," etc. similar to many of the maxims transmitted to us from the Ancients? Moreover, does not a commandment like "In everything do to others as you would have them do to you" (Matt. 7:12) also arise from a human ethics in the sense that it is the human being who provides its principle and its end? For it is what I would like, me, a human being — what I want others to do for me — that is supposed to define the principle of my conduct in regard to them, becoming the maxim of my action, as Kant would say. Everything at stake is identified with humans, those who want, or proceeds from them — what they want, what they must "do unto others" — as defined according to them. This is a system of humanism, a human wisdom. And could one not say the same about this even better-known saying: "Do not judge, so that you may not be judged" (Matt. 7:1)? In this case, it is what can happen to me, namely being judged, that decides the principle of my conduct: not to judge.

Other words nevertheless tell a completely different story. One reads in Matthew (7:11): "If you then, who are evil. . . ." Christ here still speaks to humans, in fact, to all of them. The categorical and extreme judgment on them by him who gave them the advice not to judge does not concern a category of particular individuals, guilty of reprehensible actions. Human nature is disqualified as a whole. What we have taken hastily as a system deriving its coherence from a common nature is separated irrevocably, causing disquieting questions to crop up. Must not precepts, bits of advice, pieces of information, or commandments given to humans in order to restore harmony in their relations with the world and peace amongst themselves, be in the first place appropriate to their nature — having a hold on it so as to permit its free expression, indeed its modification or its progressive amelioration? Is not the peculiar feature of all wisdom sayings to resort to observation and experience in which the interpretation of the human condition and its potentialities becomes possible, and in which ethics is given as a task for its realization? "Become what you are." Yet how could such an evolution prevail over any worth if the goal one assigns to it is itself devoid of value? How could humanism claim to establish wisdom if this wisdom has to fit a perverted reality? How could one ground an ethics on what is bad in itself? In this way a gap between what Christ says and what we think spontaneously of ourselves in our daily existence and the fulfillment of our tasks, is opened and will become enlarged to a yawning width.

As soon as one refrains from isolating them arbitrarily from their context, Christ's words, far from offering themselves to us as a species of wisdom (and especially of human wisdom), become rather its ruthless critique. What they aim at, supposing one can consider them an ethics, is not the progressive improvement of a human nature in accordance with everything we call nature in general: that of the universe, outside nature — this "outside" which Christ declared had never had any evil. This is the case because human nature is marked by an evil which is held in the heart. Not improvement but complete transformation is required. A transformation so radical that it properly signifies a change of nature, a sort of transubstantiation. The new nature which must be substituted for it can only result from a new generation. Or rather from a re-generation — in the sense of a new birth.

It is hence indispensable to recognize the importance of such a rupture with the set of laws which ordinarily rule human conduct, as well as the violence with which it is affirmed by Christ. The emotional and practical modes according to which relations among members of the same family are established are so spontaneous that one calls them "natural," which in this instance means in conformity with human nature and, consequently, in the nature of the human couple and of the family which it generates. Human relations are hence human par excellence because they seem dictated by life and by deep needs. Responding to these, they set up an equilibrium and establish the stable element on which any community rests. Since this equilibrium is originally affective, it is lived as such, as a well-being and a peace that the wisdom which claims to obtain them only helps to recognize after the fact. This is the final reason why this wisdom is called a humanism, because it only helps to attend to tendencies inscribed in what, under the term "human nature," refers to nothing other than our life.

These almost inconceivable statements [of Jesus] literally advocate the rupture of these natural and living relations: "Do not think that I have come to bring peace to the earth; I have not come to bring peace, but a sword. For I have come to set a man against his father, and a daughter against her mother, and a daughter-in-law against her mother-in-law;

23

and one's foes will be members of one's own household" (Matt. 10:34-36). The following verses from Luke (12:51-53) echo this: "Do you think that I have come to bring peace to the earth? No, I tell you, but rather division! From now on, five in one household will be divided, three against two and two against three; they will be divided: father against son, and son against father, mother against daughter and daughter against mother."

Such proposals — which pronounce the dissolution of links that have always united living beings in order to substitute discord and confrontation in their place — are far from isolated and far from concerned only with the family. Social organization as a whole is from now on not only dislocated but completely ruined. According to the strange parable of the workers in the vineyard, those who have been hired at the end of the afternoon and have only worked one hour still receive the same salary as those enlisted early in the morning who have endured the burden and heat of the day. As the famous statement claims: "The last will be first and the first will be last" (Matt. 20:1-16).

This reversal of the situation that affects social and economic existence inevitably entails that of any justice. Growing like a fire that devours everything, the subversion extends successively to different levels of experience in order finally to strike the human condition in its very essence. After the drastic reversal of all hierarchies, "the greatest among you must become like the youngest, and the leader like one who serves," "for all who exalt themselves will be humbled, but all who humble themselves will be exalted" (Luke 22:24-27 and 18:14). It is indeed the grounding of our condition in its most intimate reality, where our real life beats and is experienced. This life is prey to a sort of cataclysm so unexpected that at the moment it is for us as impossible to describe as to comprehend: "For those who want to save their life will lose it, and those who lose their life will save it" [Luke 9:24].

Yet this disconcerting situation where all is turned upside down is not expressed solely in scattered and unorganized propositions. Rather, they make way for systematic developments. Paradoxes, like many challenges to good sense, are arranged side by side in such a way that, if not one of them agreed with our thought, a mysterious affinity nevertheless seems to unite them. Readers of the Beatitudes find themselves in the presence of true speech, whether in Matthew's version or in Luke's. It is

24

as if behind this mass of unlikely propositions, a different Reason was at work, another Logos that, in order to run counter to everything humans say or think themselves, nevertheless reaches at the core of their being. As if this Word, far from being strange to our true reality, was not only linked to it according to a suitability that still escapes us, but was consubstantial with it. A key would then exist for comprehending Christ's enigmatic teaching. This key does not arise from some esoteric knowledge, from archaic mythologies, or absurd cosmogonies; it would be held hidden within us. It alone would be capable of introducing us to knowledge about ourselves.

In order to grasp this key, we must first recognize that the place circumscribed by the paradoxes of the Beatitudes *is precisely nothing other than the human condition.* It is thus really the words of Christ addressed to humans *about themselves* which are in question. Only the analysis of these words can furnish us with the principle of intelligibility for which we search.

Is it then not advisable to wonder why these words which appear as so many incomprehensible paradoxes, if not to say close to the absurd, are still not perceived as mind games like certain sophisms dear to ancient thought, but immediately felt and lived by us in their splendor and their tragic truth? Because, as we have been led to recognize on several occasions, these words run counter to the idea that we spontaneously form about ourselves and yet, at the same time, they kindle in us the acute awareness of the fragility of that idea. As we take up this reflexive sense of ourselves as beings of the world, our actions prove what they are and what we are in this world. The extraordinary criticism of hypocrisy has discredited the universe of exterior appearances in our own eyes, making us understand that the reality of the truth of our actions is not confined to it — nor is that of our flesh or our life. Reality and truth are held within us, in this flesh, in this life.

This displacement of the realty of the visible field to that of the invisible illuminates a certain number of paradoxes already encountered. The disqualification of the world in which humans place their confidence, its reduction to an appearance and, what is more, to a mendacious appearance, explains why it becomes possible to say: the one who prays does not actually pray, the one who fasts does not fast, the one who gives alms is totally uninterested in the poor as well as in the empty donation with which he favors them. It is the totality of human activities and of relations based on them which, emptying themselves of their substance, collapse into derision.

As we have pointed out, philosophical thought is nevertheless capable of protesting against the temptation of common sense, which situates all reality in the visible world. In Descartes' cogito for example, in Kant's or Husserl's "transcendental I," or even in the soul of the tradition, this reality is well and truly consigned to the realm of the invisible. One may say that these philosophical concepts themselves obey an inspiration of Christian origin. It makes no difference: with the development of philosophy, it is humans themselves, in an effort of thought which is specific to them, who manage to unblock illusions of naive objectivism or materialism, in order to understand themselves in truth.

To someone who scrutinizes Christ's words with more attention, it appears that the paradoxes do not result only from the contrast of the visible to the invisible or from the latter's belonging to our real life. *It is at the interior of this life, among the modes experienced by it, within its own feelings, that the disconcerting relation announced by Christ in the Beatitudes occurs:* "Happy are those who mourn . . . , those who hunger and thirst. . . . Happy are you when people revile you and persecute you and utter all kinds of evil against you falsely" (Matt. 5:4, 6, 10, 11). We find the same sort of puzzling affirmations in Luke's version: "Happy are you who are poor . . . you who are hungry, you who weep. . . . Happy are you when people hate you, and when they exclude you, revile you, and defame you. . . . Rejoice in that day and leap for joy" (Luke 6:20-23). In Luke's version, four curses follow on these beatitudes: "But woe to you who are rich . . . , to you who are full now . . . , to you who are laughing. . . . Woe to you when all speak well of you" (24-25).

This general subversion of all our feelings extends also to the logic inherent in them. How indeed could happiness be identical to the painful sensations of hunger or thirst, to sufferings endured during persecution, to the slights of slander; or indeed the discomfort of poverty, of tears, of hatred, of insults, or of humiliations which the contempt of others stirs up in us?

But this upheaval of the internal logic of all our affects implies in its turn that of the totality of connections which humans spontaneously establish among each other. Now this reversal is explicit. In Luke: "Love your enemies, do good to those who hate you, bless those who curse you, pray for those who abuse you. If anyone strikes you on the cheek, offer the other also; and from anyone who takes away your coat do not withhold even your shirt. Give to everyone who begs from you; and if anyone takes away your goods, do not ask for them again" [Luke 6:27-31].

Christ formulates the internal upheaval of these affects and of affective relationships not only in this abrupt presentation that, for all its paradox, still imparts a sort of fascination. Its consequences are also displayed in all clarity: habitual and natural human relationships are not only reversed but they are disqualified, judged, condemned. And here is the condemnation: "If you love those who love you, what credit is that to you? For even sinners love those who love them. If you do good to those who do good to you, what credit is that to you? For even sinners do the same. If you lend to those from whom you hope to receive, what credit is that to you? Even sinners lend to sinners, to receive as much again. But love your enemies, do good, and lend, expecting nothing in return" (Luke 6:32-34).

In this final clause of the sentence which runs the risk of going unnoticed, an essential characteristic of human relations emerges on which we have not yet reflected and which will constitute — this is the paradox — the reason for their condemnation by Christ: *reciprocity.* It is nevertheless this reciprocity which most often sets up these relationships, at the same time as it justifies them and assures them their solidity. On the most trivial level, does one not observe that these reciprocal duties, for example between neighbors or at work, give rise to connections of sympathy or of friendship? The more the role of reciprocity increases, the more do relations acquire a lasting, emotional character, which makes them natural, beneficial, specifically "human." Is it not natural and human to love those who love you? Do men not love their wives and wives their husbands, mothers their children, children their parents? Even if the connection, when extended to a larger community, loses its intensity, assuming the form of simple charity, of solidarity, of collaboration, it is still reciprocity which ensures the coherence of the group which it shapes. Affectivity and reciprocity go together to the point where the absence of reciprocity greatly impacts affectivity. A love that is not loved in return engenders tragedy.

Because social relations *are* the relations between individuals, deriving from them their substance in life (unlike "objective" relations receiving their reality from the light of the world), they manifest everywhere within them this reciprocity without which they would not be possible. We have already alluded to the economy. Now the phenomenon at the origin of economy is exchange, a concept impossible to formulate without reciprocity, since in exchange each exchanger expects and receives from the other the equivalent of what he or she gives to the other. The entire market economy, of which capitalism is only one mode, relies on exchange. All these economic phenomena, more generally all social phenomena, in turn give rise to a set of laws which seem to govern their functioning, even though they are only its ideal expression. In the agreement that accompanies each form of exchange, reciprocity is displayed in its purest form.

It is true that, like everything that is handed over to objectivity, reciprocity can fall victim to hypocrisy and deceit, or simple illusion. But as much as, on the economic level, for example, reciprocity of exchange between work and a salary that is supposed to be the equivalent in money can be but a deception, giving rise to the "exploitation" of the worker, the lived experience of reciprocal services, feelings, of reciprocal gifts as in a couple, is less likely to lend itself to this sort of manipulation. Because we have recognized the reality of life experienced immediately such as it is, the realm of the invisible — where suffering is suffering and joy is joy — no longer allows any space for deceit. Human relations here become manifest once again as real relations, assured by themselves, taking their impetus from them. One knows that one receives as much as one gives, that one gives as much as one receives. In the lived experience of this reciprocity, love becomes kindled. Returned to its life and its invincible certainty, reciprocity acquires all its force. It is when reciprocity is thus returned to life and to its certainty that it becomes natural to love those who love you. Affectivity and reciprocity go again together, communicating their force to the communities that they support and which constitute the structure of any society.

We are now in a position to perceive the hidden significance of reciprocity. Since it is always established between human beings, it is to them that it returns. It is this reciprocity between humans which justifies what they do and what they are. *What humans do, what they are, is thus made clear by starting from themselves.* It is in this manner that there is a human system because humans are situated on both sides of the relation that links them to themselves and for which they accordingly serve as the foundation. All relations that are connected between humans find their origin in them — in their nature — and this is quite right. And besides, how could it be otherwise?

Therefore, the reversal of these relations — even when they draw their strength from a real reciprocity, when they appear as "human," "natural," well-meaning or moving as those of husbands and their wives, of parents and their children, etc. — such a reversal would become properly incomprehensible, the motivation for their condemnation even more enigmatic. In the name of what or who could such relations be broken and denounced? Is it not the human condition itself, from which these relations proceed, and of which they form the framework, which would have to be placed in question, turned upside down? It is precisely this radical upheaval that Christ's word effects when, being addressed to humans, it speaks to them about themselves.

CHAPTER 3

Upheaval of the Human Condition Through Christ's Word

If one considers again the words of Christ on which we have just reflected, with even more attention, in particular those which formulate paradoxes, a first impression is confirmed. These declarations which run counter to the idea that we form about ourselves do not result only from the opposition of visible to invisible, as important as this opposition might be. Neither do they result from the sole affirmation that it is in the invisible that our true reality resides — the reason this reality is referred to as the "secret." At the interior of the invisible itself where we reside, the words of Christ trace a new line of separation which identifies its most profound dimension within the same life. Only Christ's revelation of this layer of our life, buried and doubly unnoticed by us, comes to shatter our human condition to the point that it actually ceases to be human, properly speaking. This new qualification of our life which overthrows it completely stems from what "God sees in secret." In this way, this secret which turned each one of us into a being withdrawn from the gaze of others, from the light and the "glory" of the world, a self protected by a sort of metaphysical incognito and rendered independent by it, which a certain classical ethics had understood as an inviolate conscience, in reality is nothing of the sort. Or rather, it is such, a guarded mystery, an "inviolate conscience," only precisely in its connection with others, as far as, withdrawn from their gaze as from the light of the world, it conceals itself in the invisible. Yet in the invisible, this secret, this mysterious and impenetrable self, is crossed by another gaze which pierces it to the heart, there exactly where it is the secret. And this gaze is nothing other and nothing less than that of God.

The meaning of the critique of hypocrisy is from now on totally modified. According to our first approach, the possibility of hypocrisy is caused by the fact that, in its living reality, each self escapes the gaze of the world, not only in its thoughts but equally in its acts. In their execution these actions are invisible; only their exterior appearance gives itself as a spectacle in the form of a corporeal objective displacement, so that one can feign fasting or prayer without really praying or fasting. Yet, as the text of Matthew reinstated in its entirety, God sees in secret and, at the same time, he sees our action as it really is. "But when you give alms, do not let your left hand know what your right hand is doing, so that your alms may be done in secret . . . ; your Father sees what you do in secret." And also: "But whenever you pray, go into your room and shut the door and pray to your Father who is in secret; and your Father who sees in secret will reward you" (6:3-4, 6).

The human condition hence can no longer be defined only in terms of the opposition of the invisible and the visible, understood as an opposition of the self to the world and identified with it. Within the invisible itself, a chasm widens, a new relationship is established. The self is not linked only to the world and to others; it relates not only to itself in the secret of its thoughts and its acts. This secret is submitted to the gaze of a God. In this way, by this gaze which reveals humans to themselves and at the same time reveals them to God, they are linked to God in this interior relationship which now defines their reality. *In this way the human condition finds itself turned upside down at the very moment when it no longer receives its being from the light of the world in which men and women face each other, fighting for their prestige, but from the interior relationship to God and from the revelation in which this new and fundamental relationship consists.*

Christ's words recounted in the Gospels will permit us to understand gradually the nature of this relationship in which the joint revelation of the secret between the human and God and between self and self is fulfilled. Let us restrict ourselves for the moment to noticing how the new definition of the human condition clarifies the most disconcerting paradoxes, giving a decisive meaning to what seems not to have any. At stake is the reversal or rather the rupture of the living and spontaneous relations which unite members of the same family. Let us keep in mind the texts in Matthew and Luke: "Yes, I have come to set a man against his father, and a daughter against her mother." "Do you think that I have come to bring peace to the earth? No, I tell you, but rather division! From now on five in one household will be divided, three against two and two against three" (respectively, Matt. 10:34-35 and Luke 12:51-53). And from this, as we have seen, come all the consequences of a general critique of the law of reciprocity of feelings in human relations. This reciprocity requires, for example, that we love those who love us or that we feel hostility, if not hatred, toward those who hate us. Hence the contrary instruction formulated by Christ, certainly difficult to understand, even more difficult to observe: "Love your enemies."

We are now in a position to understand at what the radical challenging of reciprocity aims. It is because of nothing other than the terms of this relationship, namely humans, that reciprocity in human relations is dismissed with such vehemence. Based on reciprocity and explained by it, human relationship seems autonomous and self-sufficient. It exists for itself, that is to say, for the sake of the humans among whom it is established. And it is likewise self-explained by the nature of these humans — by human nature. The supposed independence of human relationship resting on reciprocity which everywhere places men, women, children, and parents at the origin of this relation, neglects nothing less than the interior relation of the human being to God — a relation unfolded in secret and which we will see grounds human existence as surely as its intelligibility. It is the truth of the human condition and, as a result, that of all of the connections that human beings are capable of fostering among themselves which are completely concealed.

How does Christ condemn the reciprocity which makes up the fabric of the most common human relationships, bestowing on them this "natural" character, from which they obtain their justification in the eyes of all — this reciprocity which makes us love those who love us, as though by an invincible force? Why, to our amazement, does Christ brandish the broadsword which comes to sever these familiar ties where life searches and finds its fulfillment and its joy? How? By a radical affirmation of non-reciprocity. Why this affirmation? *Because non-reciprocity is the decisive feature of the new fundamental relationship that we have just discovered, the interior and hidden relationship between humans and God, more exactly between God and humans.* The divine word does indeed flash like a broadsword: "Love your enemies, do good, and lend, *expecting nothing in return.* Your reward will be great, and you will be children of the Most High; for *he is kind to the ungrateful and the wicked*" (Luke 6:35; emphasis mine).

Luke first formulates God's relation to humans under the light of goodness, the goodness that Matthew also invokes: "for he makes his sun rise on the evil and on the good" (5:45). Pondering the light of goodness, the word seems to consist of an ethical dictate, actually showing how to conduct oneself toward others. No longer according to the spontaneous natural law of reciprocity, rendering good for good, but also evil for evil, hostility or vengeance for insult or harm suffered. According to the new word, returning good for evil is to act in such a way that the so-called natural relationships are destroyed and the ancient law (eye for eye, tooth for tooth) is overthrown.

Yet, the word says something more than the reversal of human relationships, as important as that is. It only leads to this, wreaking division and discord where harmony and reciprocal love reigned, because it first turns the human condition upside down. The reason for this is that this condition is no longer defined on the human plane by the system of reciprocal relationships between humans but by the interior relation of each one among them to God. It is because the human condition is constituted by the relationship to God that these relations of human beings amongst themselves can no longer obey human criteria and prescriptions by drawing their origin from a supposed human nature that no longer exists. A passage of profound density implies this change of nature, this transubstantiation of a human nature into a nature generated in God, divine in its principle and whose actions can henceforth only be discovered by this divine principle and origin: "Do good, and lend, expecting nothing in return . . . *and you will be sons of the Most High*"; "Pray for those who persecute you, *so that you may be sons of your Father in heaven*" (Luke 6:35; Matt. 5:44, respectively; emphasis mine).

A thesis that will be at the center of Christianity hence emerges from the paradoxes that extend those of the Beatitudes and concern the reversal of human relations: "You are the sons of God." This new definition of the human condition in the texts of Luke and Matthew — in contrast to any social or humanist interpretation — is future-oriented and seems dependent on future fulfillment. The condition of "son" calls for an action on our part, a difficult action because it runs counter to an instinctive spontaneity. Such an action nevertheless does not derive its merit from its difficulty, from the enigmatic obstacle that it is necessary to surmount. It is prefigured by the manner in which God acts toward us, he who ignores the pettiness of reciprocity, who is good to the ungrateful and the wicked. Does not God's manner of acting toward us in this way offer itself as the model of behavior that must be ours in regard to our fellow men, the principle of an *imitatio Dei* which would render us more demanding and better in our ordinary conduct, worthy at the end of these efforts to be called "the sons of the Most High"?

That would be to underestimate the range of the Word addressed to us. God's action on our behalf is in no way limited to serving as a model for our attitude toward him. The non-reciprocity to which it witnesses is impossible to be understood on the human plane, where it would be reduced to a simple negation of the reciprocity which characterizes natural relations, as if, ceasing to love those who love us, we were to start being hostile to them. Or as if, ceasing to be hostile to our enemies, we begin to love them, as if by a miracle. The non-reciprocity of the interior relationship that links us to God signifies the intervention of a different relationship than those established between humans, taking its point of departure in us, finding in them the cause of its trials. *Non-reciprocity indicates the immanent generation of our finite Life in the infinite Life of God.* It takes its meaning from the internal process of that absolute and infinite Life of God himself. For in the internal process of this infinite Life each living being is provided in its own life in such a way that the relationship between this living being and the Life that makes it live in fact is unaware of any reciprocity. The designation "sons of God" that is conferred on us through the entire Gospel is not a metaphor; it describes our real condition. If in the text on which we comment the status of sons that is conferred on us is a matter of becoming that for which the conditions are fixed with precision, it is because it is for us a matter of recovering our original condition which has been denatured, forgotten, but never abolished.

That is the way in which one must understand this irrevocable declaration by Christ: "Call no one your father on earth, for you have one Father — the one in heaven" (Matt. 23:9). No one on earth should call another man his father, not because there would be a hesitation about the person in principle, but because no man on earth can claim this title. This is because there is in fact only one sole Father, he who is in heaven and who is God. Any human being is a son of God and of God alone. And the reason for this "radical" situation which concerns the root of the human, is the following: no living being has the power to bring him- or herself forth into life; nor does a living being know how to sustain this life from another living being like it, as powerless as itself, equally incapable of giving itself life. Only an all-powerful Life holding the capacity for bringing itself into life — this unique and absolute Life which is that of God — can communicate its breath to those it has made to live and who are from then on, in a real and itself absolute sense, "sons."

Yet, if no human on earth has any other man as father, in turn no human is anyone else's father: properly speaking, no one can be called son or father. Henceforth, all terrestrial links and especially familial relations become in some sense emptied of their substance, deprived of the actuality that we attribute to them communally. The extraordinary question of the reality or the validity of the set of his or her relations hence is posed to each living being in an unexpected fashion — the question of knowing who is his or her father but also who is his or her mother, who is his brother, his sister, maybe her son or her daughter. This is an extraordinary question since it is from now on possible that it remain without answer. And this is certainly the stunning question Christ asks when he is told that his mother and his brothers are there and want to see him: "A crowd was sitting around him; and they said to him, 'Your mother and your brothers and sisters are outside, asking for you.' And he replied: 'Who are my mother and my brothers?' And looking at those who sat around him, he said, 'Here are my mother and my brothers! Whoever does the will of God is my brother and sister and mother'" (Mark 3:32-35; cf. Matt. 12:48-50).

Yet this at first so shocking dissolution of familial relationships makes possible the division between the members of one family. Christ affirmed that this was his mission in a passage already encountered. "I have not come to bring peace but war, separating a man from his father, a daughter from her mother." This division is difficult to accept or even incomprehensible — that was one of the many paradoxes — but which becomes conceivable once the reality of these family connections has been contested or, rather, denied. And this is the case, actually in a radical manner, when human natural genealogy is purely and simply disqualified in favor of the divine genealogy which alone makes of each one of them the son of God.

Separated from him who appears as his or her father in the eyes of the world, in the understanding and according to the explanations of this world, separated in the same fashion from her who, in the same world and according to its explanations, would appear as his or her mother — and even of those who are or would be said to be his or her brothers, sisters, sons or daughters — nevertheless does not leave the human adrift, deprived of any identity, detached from anything, lost as in Rossellini's film *Paisa* where the bodies of the resistance fighters laid on life rafts approach the sea carried by the waves of the Po. Following on the brutal rupture of familial relations, on the general destruction of human relationships, comes without transition their reconstruction according to the divine order. This is the order which recognizes in principle only one Father, in such a way that all humans are his sons and that the only real relationship which subsists in this new order — to the exclusion of any distinction, separation, or opposition — is that of brothers and sisters.

This is the first essential revelation brought to humans by Christ, when he speaks to them about themselves in their own language: You are the sons of God. You have only one sole and same Father. You are connected by relationships which unite all those who have the same Father and who, in this manner, are brothers. These relationships in no way constitute an ideal, nor do they result from a law which one could either observe or transgress. Even less is it permitted to see in them nothing more than a metaphor. Christ here reveals to us the actual reality of relationships which unite all human beings. Such relations can no longer be understood starting from the social image that humans forge for themselves, after their manner of seeing: the manner in which one introduces oneself according to one's education, the civilization or culture to which one belongs. The relationships of brothers which exist among humans are their real relationships because the reality of each one among them is that of being a son of God and this one God is the Father of all.

How then can we not observe that the non-reciprocity between the absolute Life of God and the life of each of the living beings to which it gives Life — of which it is the life — creates a new reciprocity among them? This reciprocity no longer results from the fact that the human beings among whom it is established have the same nature, a human nature. It results from the interior relationship of each living being to the Life in which it lives; and, in this manner, from the interior relationship that it has, in this Life, with each one of the other living beings who draw their own life from this same Life — which is his or hers and which is theirs, which is their life in common. This interior relationship of all the living beings to one another in the same Life in which each lives and which lives in each is none other than the new reciprocity founded by Christ, the one which makes of each man and each woman a brother and a sister for his or her brother and sister.[1]

It is nevertheless a good idea to underline that the new reciprocity founded by Christ has nothing to do with the reciprocity at work in the so-called natural relations. Because this latter was established among human beings understood as such, the system of relations that it upholds can be considered a human system. Yet it is far from lending itself to the idyllic description that one usually fabricates about it and which does not match up even for the restricted and privileged group, the family. Limited to its human reference, is reciprocity not often hostility in all its shapes: competition, rivalry, antagonism of ambitions and interests, pretence, intrigue, lying, resentment, hatred, violence, aggression, and finally war? When these conflicting relationships exhaust themselves, do they not make way for indifference? Even passion itself changes into indifference. In fact, although these human relationships are not ruled by objective relations — financial, economic, or others — and when to the contrary they "come from the heart," they fall even more under Christ's judgment according to which "it is from the heart that all evil comes forth." And here is where this judgment strikes love equally, as long as, ruled by the human law of reciprocity, it is confined to making us love those who love us.

1. [The gender inclusiveness here is Henry's own. — Trans.]

That "the pagans do the same," according to the declaration repeated by Christ, carries the condemnation to the extreme, at the same time as it enlightens its final motivation. For pagans do not know God. Love completely dissolves itself in the absence of God, dependent upon the love of the other as the love of the other is dependent upon mine, risky in the same way as the reciprocity to which it owes its evanescent existence. Love, in fact, is just another name for life and our own love functions like our own life. My love cannot rest solely on that of another just as another's cannot rely on mine — any more than my life can be grounded on the life of another or another's grounded on mine. The foundation of any love, the foundation of life, collapses under the demands of alternating realities, albeit symmetrical, none of which is sufficient unto itself or carries this foundation in itself. Reciprocity is here the mark of nothingness. This absurdity of human relationship reduced to itself, this absurdity which is nothing other than the negation of God and which constitutes blasphemy, stirs up Christ's rage. The paradoxes of the Beatitudes are the equivalent of the passionate declaration: *Abba,* Father!

This is the reason why the Kingdom of God arises from the paradox and its affirmation. "Happy are you who are poor, for yours is the kingdom of God" (Luke 6:20). "Happy are those who are persecuted . . . for theirs is the kingdom of heaven" (Matt. 5:10). "Happy are you when people hate you, and when they exclude you, revile you and defame you . . . for surely your reward is great in heaven" (Luke 6:22-23). "Happy are you when people revile you and persecute you and utter all kinds of evil against you. . . . Rejoice and be glad, for your reward is great in heaven" (Matt. 5:11-12). The relationship of the paradox to the Kingdom is constant; it remains even when it is not explicitly named but signified by one of its properties. These are properties which, although they are not those that theology traditionally attributes to God, nevertheless tell us of his Kingdom in an infinitely more suggestive fashion. "Satisfaction," "laughing," "consolation," "forgiveness," "vision of God," "rejoicing," "cheerfulness" — this is what the Kingdom gives and what comes to satisfy the great Desire of humans, to accomplish their interior relation to God.

Yet not only does this interior relationship which makes the human being the son of God turn upside down the set of relationships that human beings have with one another. As regards the life of each one, it makes new paradoxes appear that are explicitly formulated in the Beatitudes, to which we have not yet accorded sufficient attention. According to the definition that I have proposed, life is what is experienced in itself, immediately and without distance. It reveals itself, that is to say it reveals itself to itself or, as one can also say in philosophical terms, it is self-revelation [*auto-révélation*]. This essential property of life is found in each of its modalities. The peculiarity of suffering, for example, is to experience itself. If one asks: who can help us know our suffering? one must answer: it is itself. If one asks: what does our suffering make known to us? one must answer again: what it tell us, is itself. For suffering reveals itself to us in its own affectivity, in its impressionable flesh. And it is thus with each one of our joys, of our sorrows, of our desires or of our troubles, of our anguish or of our hope. This insuperable certainty specific to each of the impressions we feel, provided that we stick to what we actually experience (the fact that, for example, it is impossible to doubt our pain or our pleasure so long as we really experience them), is what causes the most paradoxical characteristic of all the paradoxes of the Beatitudes. It is so paradoxical in fact that it struck me during my first encounter with these exceptional texts. For finally, I ask, how can one be happy if one is hungry — or when one cries, or endures insults and persecutions? Or how can the sorrow that makes us weep be, in itself, the pleasure that we experience in laughing? Is it possible to refer here to our relation to God? As interior to all our suffering and to each offense borne, does this relation to God change their nature in an incomprehensible fashion, operating as a sort of magical transformation of suffering into joy, for example?

We are not yet in a position to respond to these questions. Without doubt one must know more about our relation to God, examine many other words of Christ which would explain it to us. Before pursuing this examination, let me return to one of my preliminary remarks. The words Christ speaks to humans in their language do not all speak about them. The most essential and surprising ones speak about him, about Christ, who speaks to them. Yet our relation to God, which turns human relations and the very condition of being human upside down — this relationship on which all depends — depends itself on what Christ says of himself and of his own status. We must therefore now examine the words of Christ about himself.

CHAPTER 4

Words That Christ Addresses to Humans in Their Own Language — No Longer about Them, but about Himself: Affirmation of His Divine Status

The few words of Christ on which we have concentrated our attention until now were sufficient to produce what had to be called a disruption of the relationships that humans maintain with each other, as well as of the human condition itself. The pattern of this generalized subversion derived from placing in question the reciprocity at work in these relationships. Yet reciprocity was itself denounced for a more profound reason. Being established between terms — men, women, fathers, mothers, sons, daughters, etc. — who are all human beings, reciprocity made of them the real bases of this intersubjective network which forms the "human world." Accordingly, the human being with its own nature, human nature, was posited as the foundation of this world. In this version of things, the human condition appears autonomous, sufficient unto itself, developing a world or a "society" which is the expression of this sufficiency and of this autonomy.

The passionate affirmation of non-reciprocity which characterizes the relation of the human being to God — who is good to the ungrateful and the wicked — is accompanied by the unconditional affirmation of this relationship. Consequently, far from being autonomous, the human condition consists in this interior relationship to God; it only exists within it, is only understood by it. This is what non-reciprocity means: *the immanence of the absolute Life of each living being.* This is the life which alone has the power to give life to itself and consequently of giving it to all the living. Christ calls this all-powerful Life "the Father." This is why he says to humans: "You have only one Father, he who is in heaven."

"In heaven" obviously does not mean: in interstellar space, in the astrophysical universe explored by the cosmonauts who, looking out from the windows of their spacecraft, did not see God. "In heaven" means: in the invisible life in which all living beings live, in which they are themselves invisible, just like this life. This is the new definition of the human being and of its true condition, that of a living being engendered in the invisible and absolute Life of God. This Life remains in them as long as they live and outside of it no living being can stand upright. This is why they are called "sons of God," of this absolute Life which gives the gift of life to them without cease.[1]

It is by virtue of this new definition of the human condition — because, as sons of God, humans have only one Father — that all the human, familial, professional, social, etc. relationships find themselves in turn subverted for the benefit of completely new relationships. They are no longer relationships among autonomous beings, free to follow the natural course of their impulses — of love toward those who love them, of hostility toward those who are hostile to them. It is a matter of relationships among beings predestined by their interior relationship which each of them maintains with God. From now on everyone, predestined in him- or herself by this relationship, is referred to another who is predestined in the same fashion. Such is, as we have seen, the new reciprocity of relationships among those who, sons and daughters of the same Father, are originally and in themselves brothers and sisters, whatever would be the motives of attraction or of repulsion which continue to govern the ancient Law surreptitiously.

With this new definition of the human condition and consequently the relationships which it implies, Christ's Word accomplishes *the substitution of a divine genealogy for a natural genealogy.* And this substitution concerns humans as much as him who comes to teach it to them in a teaching so fundamental that one must really call it a revelation. It is a revelation of what they are — sons of the same God — and hence of what they must do: love each other as is proper for children of the same father. From this revelation results not only what we have called the reversal of

---

1. [The final phrase of this sentence could also be translated as "which makes them without cease the gift of life." — Trans.]

the conception of human nature but its complete abolishment. There is no human nature, as there is no human in the sense in which we have always understood it: that is, a human being having its own nature, proper to humans and belonging to them, a "human nature." Human beings are nothing other than sons of God. Their origin is held in God, their nature arises out of that of God. Engendering humans as living beings, giving them a life which exists in himself, God has in this way given them the same nature as his own: that of life. It is in this way that God has made humanity in his own image and likeness (Gen. 1:26).

Let me open a brief parenthesis. According to Christian theology Christ's nature is twofold, divine and human at the same time. As regards his human nature, it is advisable to understand it not as one habitually does but as that of a living being generated in the divine Life and holding from it its own life. Put differently, in regard to Christ considered as a human being it is indispensable to accomplish the substitution of the divine genealogy for the natural genealogy — a divine genealogy which Christ comes to reveal to humans as constituting their true nature. It is here that Christ's word spoken to humans about themselves reflects back on him, who addressed this word to them. But this is only a first indication.

For here a question arises that cannot be postponed. In what one calls "Jesus' inaugural speech,"[2] Christ offers humans an extraordinary revelation about themselves, unveiling for them their true reality. In regard to this so far unthought reality, he has drawn consequences that are no less extraordinary, denouncing their most natural and dearest human relationships. He has formulated incomprehensible propositions about everyone's life, calling happy those who are in distress, identifying joy and suffering, laughing and tears with each other. Yet, all these assertions are not presented as exhortations, entreaties, commandments of an ethical nature, even less as a wise man's maxims or counsels for the comfort of a poor suffering humanity. Their categorical formulation, their irrefutable tone, and the formal character of the circumstances that surround what is no longer a sermon but really a sacred Revelation make of these amazing words so many absolute truths.

2. In the "Index suivant l'ordre chronologique," in *Synopse des Quatres Évangiles*, M. J. Lagrange, C. Lavergne (Paris: Librairie Lecoffre, 1999), 67-76.

From this results the inevitable question, as a backward surge of the gaze looking away from those to whom Revelation is made toward him who utters it: how does he know all that? Who is he to possess such knowledge? It is in this way that Christ's words speaking to humans about their condition of being human inevitably revert to him and put him severely into question, summoning him to justify these so disconcerting remarks — which he cannot do without justifying himself. And the more Christ proceeds in the analysis of the human condition toward its hidden relationship in God, the more his statements will grow increasingly distant from what humans, whether they are educated or not, presume to know about themselves. The more they show the mysteries of a divine Life to be linked in all human existence, the more the question — pressing, urgent, menacing — will redound on him, on what he claims to know or to be.

Does Christ not know too much for a human being? Just sticking to the words already encountered, they do not sound only like those of an initiate or a prophet. Upon reflection one must ask oneself whether an initiate or a prophet, even if the greatest of prophets, would be in a position to formulate them. Since he announces that the poor will be in possession of the Kingdom of God, must he not know what this Kingdom is? And the Kingdom comes up continually in the Beatitudes and the curses. It appears in an explicit form, when it is said of the pure of heart that "they will see God," the peacemakers that "they will be called the sons of God," those persecuted for justice, that "the kingdom belongs to them." It appears in an implicit form inasmuch as, according to a remark by Father Lagrange, "in the biblical style, verbs in the passive absolute often point out the action of God" — as is the case in the Beatitudes where "they will be satisfied" means "they will be satisfied by God," "they will be consoled," "they will be consoled by God." Christ must know not only the nature of the Kingdom but the relationship of human life to this Kingdom, the modalities of this life which lead there (poverty, purity, sweetness, hunger, hunger and thirst for justice, etc.), and the connection which unites them in the work of salvation which they render possible.

Yet the one who delivers the Beatitudes does not only know all that — the nature of the Kingdom, of our relation to it according to our manner of living, inclusion in the case of modalities which have just been cited, or exclusion in the case of richness, of well-being, of the glory which the world gives — *he himself intervenes in this relationship.* It is he who opens the doors of the Kingdom to those who recognize him and who accept hatred, insults, and persecution *on his behalf*: "Blessed are you when people hate you, and when they exclude you, revile you and defame you *on account of the Son of Man.* Rejoice in that day and leap for joy, for surely your reward is great in heaven." "Blessed are you when people revile you and persecute you and utter all kinds of evil against you falsely *on my account.* Rejoice and be glad, for your reward is great in heaven" (Luke 6:22-23; Matt. 5:11-12; emphasis mine). Yet, if it is Christ himself who opens or closes the door to the Kingdom depending on whether a person will recognize him and speak his name before humans or, being ashamed of him and of his name, will reject him, is that not because he himself constitutes the access to the Kingdom because he is the Gate — *the relation to God as such?* Yet who would have the audacity to claim such power for himself, namely that of leading to God? What man could do so? To lead to God, to clear the path which gives access to the Kingdom: is that not to accomplish the revelation of God? And who can accomplish the revelation of God, if not God himself?

A decisive caesura is inscribed at the heart of the Beatitudes. It separates two intimately related theses in the teaching of Christ, equally essential and yet distinct. The first is the change brought to our understanding of humans, making them no longer beings of the world or of nature but sons of God. In this way the substitution of the divine genealogy of humans in place of their natural genealogy is accomplished. Such is the content of Christ's words showing to humans the reality and truth of their condition as human.

The second thesis, which will bestow on Christ's teaching its unique character in the history of religions, is implied in the first — as its presupposition. The rejection of the natural genealogy of the human leads inevitably to the gaping question of divine genealogy. If to be human — what makes a human being a human being — cannot be explained from nature or from natural elements but only from God, then it is not sufficient to affirm this divine genealogy; one must also say in what it consists. Even more: it is not sufficient to say in what it consists; *one must also be able to make it happen, to know God, to know the process by which he engenders in himself something like the human.* In this way the really abyssal question is formulated, with which Christ will inevitably find himself confronted.

The stupefying character of the Beatitudes, however, does not depend first only on the statements they formulate regarding the human condition. Behind this series of paradoxes, it is the Word they offer that fascinates us more than anything, the knowledge with which it is charged, knowledge unknown to us yet which nevertheless strikes us to the heart. It is the question which it raises. We do not wonder: What is he saying? Why does he force me to cease loving those close to me? Why should I love my enemies and if I want to do so, how can I succeed? Instead we wonder: Who speaks like this? Who is this?

This question is at the core of the Gospels. Two facts must be noted here. The first is that, despite their amazement or their fear, their fury or their dismay, Christ's contemporaries, those who heard his words, who followed him in his wanderings through the villages or in the synagogues, friends or enemies, disciples or those responsible for persecutions to come, in various shapes, openly or secretly, through hypocritical questions or veritable traps, all at some point or other will ask him that question: Who are you? What do you say about yourself? By what right do you say this or do that?

Yet (and that is the second fact) never does Christ consider this question to be untimely or unfounded. To the contrary, to his eyes as to theirs, this is a decisive question, the only one that matters. If he happens to dismiss it or to avoid it, it is for a strategic or circumstantial reason. The moment has not yet come. Those who listen are not yet in a position to understand. The scribes and Pharisees will close the net too quickly on him when they want to catch him, when his mission is not yet accomplished. Yet that, to his eyes as to theirs, the question is legitimate and even inevitable, one sees in the fact that he poses it himself to his disciples, when they do not ask him themselves or do not dare to do so, considering how frightening its stakes appear. For finally, if he is neither a human nor a prophet, nor the greatest among them, who could he be?

It is hence Christ himself who will reveal who he is. A progressive revelation, for the reasons we have just suggested, but undeniable, if one sticks to the texts. For contrary to the atheistic and mendacious exegesis

45

of the nineteenth century, it does not appear only in the late writings. It is present everywhere, in the Logia from which the Synoptic Gospels derive or in the primitive passages in John, as in the most ancient oral tradition, as Paul's letters witness. Let me show briefly the stages of this revelation.

From the beginning of his public life onward, the word Christ speaks to humans distresses by its tone and its authority. "Now when Jesus had finished saying these things, the crowds were astounded at his teaching, for he taught them as one having authority, and not as their scribes" (Matt. 7:28). Yet, the human character of him who addresses himself to humans is from the outset called into question by his very word, to the point where it establishes an apparently infinite distance between him and them: "If you then, who are evil"; "Go away from me, you evildoers" (Matt. 7:11, 23). Yet the distance thus carved out between those who are evil and him who is exempt from all evil covers a more essential difference. Christ has challenged natural generation for the benefit of a divine generation, and this for humans themselves, making them in this way sons of the one God. Thus the difference between Christ and humans must now be grasped at the interior of the divine generation itself. We have recognized in the Beatitudes how Christ suddenly places himself at the interior of the relationship which unites each human being to God, when he asserts that it will be accomplished for all those who will have suffered insult and persecution on account of him, that it is to all those that the rejoicing of the Kingdom would be given (cf. Luke 6:22-23; Matt. 5:11-12). These radical texts make explicit that the relationship to God is accomplished in Christ: "Those who are ashamed of me and of my words in this adulterous and sinful generation, of them the Son of Man will also be ashamed when he comes in the glory of his Father with the holy angels"; "Those who are ashamed of me and my words, of them the Son of Man will be ashamed when he comes in his glory and the glory of the Father and of the holy angels" (Mark 8:38; Luke 9:26).

Not only human destiny — the judgment which alone matters and which will come in the end — depends on this relationship with Christ, but this relationship with Christ would appear identical to the relationship with God; the accomplishment of the first is that of the second under its concrete form: the beatitude of the Kingdom. With a parallel judgment — which is that of the Father who sees in secret and against whom the judgment of the world has lost all power — it would actually be a matter of each person's destiny. This is what is said in the same passages where the violence of the paradox reaches its limit: "For those who want to save their life will lose it, and those who lose their life *for my sake* will save it"; "For those who want to save their life will lose it, and those who lose their life *for my sake,* and for the sake of the gospel, will save it"; "For those who want to save their life will lose it, and those who lose their life *for my sake* will find it" (Luke 9:24; Mark 8:35; Matt. 16:25; emphasis mine).

If Christ is part of the interior relationship of the human being with God to the point of identifying himself with it, hence defining the path which leads to the Kingdom, it is certainly following him that is at stake for everyone who seeks this Kingdom. Following him and for that reason giving up one's own life, the pleasures and the glory of the world, accepting the suffering included in this renunciation — suffering of which Christ's existence offers the mysterious example. From this follows, in the immediate context of the words on which we are meditating, the reiterated injunction: "Then he said to them all, 'If any want to become my followers, let them deny themselves and take up their cross daily and follow me'" (Luke 9:23; see also Matt. 16:24; Mark 8:34).

It is this intervention of Christ in the relationship with God as condition for the [divine-human] relationship which explains the new formulation of the breakdown of relations between humans. It is the presence of Christ at the interior of these connections which makes his critique more intelligible and as it were, somewhat more acceptable, hence more humane. Because, as we will see more clearly, he is the one who joins each living being to another, forming precisely the substance of the link which unites them, a preeminence Christ established at the interior of human relations — this preeminence which leads him to declare in fully logical fashion: "He who loves his father or his mother more than me is not worthy of me; he who loves his son or daughter more than me is not worthy of me." Is it simply luck, or the redactor's choice, when in Matthew's text these declarations, which place Christ at the center of the relationship to the other, are immediately followed by two fundamental statements present, as we have seen, in the other Synoptic Gospels? In the first Christ invites his disciples to follow him on the way of suffering

47

which is that of the Kingdom. "He who does not take up his cross and follow me is not worthy of me." The second indicates what being worthy of Christ means: not to want to keep one's life for oneself but to give it to Christ, for the sake of Christ — that is, to receive the life that does not die. The astonishing affirmation of Christ about himself, his identification with God, blazes out to the extreme limit of paradox, where one must lose one's life in order to keep it.

The word of Christ spoken to humans about their own human condition thus reflects back on himself. In tracing a dividing line within the divine genealogy which has implications for them as much as for him, a line which separates him off radically, he no longer presents himself as a Son among others, among all those who, having the same Father, owe life to him as well. He who has just spoken — according to the words we have just heard, and many others without doubt on which we have reflected and which carry, at bottom, the same exorbitant claim — it is he who, just as the Father does, holds the life which does not pass away: his Word [*Verbe*].

Now we must deepen the affirmation which claims that Christ has not only a human nature — in the sense he has taught us — but a divine nature.

CHAPTER 5

Christ's Words about Himself:
Reaffirmation of His Divine Status

The celebrated episode of the encounter with the Samaritan woman is one of the Gospel passages where Christ abruptly reveals his divine status. The circumstance is significant: the revelation is made to a stranger on terrain hostile to Judaism, and this precisely for a religious reason — the Samaritans have their own temple and sacrifices. Hence we must understand how this revelation was difficult for official Judaism to accept, in spite of the prophecy of the previous centuries. In this respect, it is important to observe that in the Johannine text the episode of this revelation follows immediately upon the prophecy of the Baptist. Yet it is not only a stranger, it is a sinner and obviously an unsophisticated woman to whom this message is directed. In a striking counterpoint, he who will call himself the Messiah is expressly presented in human terms.

"Jesus, tired out by his journey, was sitting by the well." He asks a drink of a woman who has come to draw water at this well of Jacob. And this is the dialogue: "How is that you, a Jew, ask a drink of me, a woman of Samaria?" Jesus answered her: "If you knew the gift of God, and who it is that is saying to you, 'Give me to drink,' you would have asked him, and he would have given you living water." The woman said to him, "Sir, you have no bucket, and the well is deep. Where do you get that living water? Are you greater than our ancestor Jacob?" Jesus said to her, "Everyone who drinks of this water will be thirsty again, but those who drink of the water that I will give them will never be thirsty" (John 4:6-14). The extraordinary dialogue, whose content is not yet completely intelligible to us, concludes with the act of faith in which the woman declares knowing

49

that "'the Messiah is coming' (who is called the Christ)" and Jesus says to her, "I am he, the one who is speaking to you" [4:25-26].

Thirst, hunger: these words which return so often in the Gospel and which we have recognized especially in the Beatitudes are only invested with such a heavy significance because they point to a finite life, the life of a flesh such as ours, which is incapable of being self-sufficient, of bringing itself into life, always in need, desiring and suffering; or, as we have said in more philosophical terms, a life which is not its own foundation. The infinite Life of God, which brings itself into life and into the enjoyment of living, is the very opposite. Carrying this omnipotence in it, it never dies. "The water that I will give will become in them a spring of water gushing up to eternal life" (John 4:14). The Messiah, the Christ, in the sense in which we understand Christ, is nothing other than and nothing less than he who, holder of eternal life, is also in a position to dispense it to whomever he would like.

It would be pointless to object to this overwhelming declaration, devoid of any ambiguity, that it is found in a late (or allegedly late) text. Even if it is here repeatedly formulated, Christ's identification with the Word of God is in no way the prerogative of John's Gospel alone. It is all over the Synoptics, either in the form of explicit statements or resulting directly from Christ's words or actions. The Beatitudes demonstrate this as much as the developments which succeed them. We have recognized that only the one who knows the Kingdom can reveal to humans the way to get there, the sacrifices to which they must consent in their life in order to crush in it all forms of idolatry and egoism and to open themselves to the divine Life, allowing themselves to be invaded by it. For the Kingdom is nothing other than the reign of this Life which knows no misfortune of finitude and of destruction. Even more, we would say, only he who knows this Kingdom of Life as well as the relationship of any finite life to it, he who *himself constitutes this relationship* of humans to God, can present himself as the savior, a constant affirmation throughout the Gospels.

In Matthew (11:27): "All things have been handed over to me by my Father; and no one knows the Son except the Father; and no one knows the Father except the Son and anyone to whom the Son chooses to reveal him." In Luke (10:22): "All things have been handed over to me by my Father; and no one knows who the Son is except the Father, or who the Father is except the Son and anyone to whom the Son chooses to reveal him." How can we not glimpse in these statements the abyss widening between Christ and humans — including the prophets — at the same time as he identifies with the Father as the only Son, an identity consisting in the reciprocal and exclusive knowledge one has of the other? Why be surprised that other and no less decisive affirmations arise in this incendiary context: "Then turning to his disciples, Jesus said to them privately, 'Blessed are the eyes that see what you see! For I tell you that many prophets and kings desired to see what you see, but did not see it, and to hear what you hear, but did not hear it'" (Luke 10:23-24; cf. also Matt. 13:16-17). He who alone knows the Father of whom he is the sole Son, and hence the Kingdom and the way which leads there, who has given power to his disciples to expel demons, can say to them, when they return to announce to him what they have done: "Do not rejoice at this, that the spirits submit to you, but rejoice that your names are written in heaven" (Luke 10:20).

After this identification with the Father of him who is thus distinguished from all humans, from all the other sons in the sense in which he alone knows the Father, his designation as "Son," encountered in the aforementioned passages of Matthew and Luke, receives then an absolutely singular meaning: it refers only to him. Limiting our investigation always to passages not contained in John, let us notice first this phrase, close to the Beatitudes: "Whoever welcomes me welcomes the one who sent me" (Matt. 10:40). Does this dazzling turn of phrase not posit the relationship of identification between Christ and his Father — a relationship still not understood by us — in all clarity? Is not the same relationship affirmed with no less force when, instead of being welcomed, Christ finds himself rejected, not only by one or another of those who accompany him but by an entire generation — and henceforth condemns it? "As Jesus came near and saw the city, he wept over it, saying: 'If you, even you, had only recognized on this day the things that make for peace! But now they are hidden from your eyes. Indeed, the days will come upon you, when your enemies will set up ramparts around you . . . they will not leave within you one stone upon another; because *you did not recognize the time of your visitation from God*'" (Luke 19:41-44; emphasis mine). The extraordinary reversal occurs here in which the man who approaches Jerusalem and sees the city with his eyes of the flesh reveals himself — at a point in space, at a moment in time, and yet hidden to the eyes of the world — as none other than the all-powerful power which rules the generations and alone gives peace: God himself.

This has reverberations in the reproaches to the cities where the majority of his miracles had taken place, because they did not convert: "Woe to you, Chorazin! Woe to you, Bethsaida! . . . And you, Capernaum, will you be exalted to heaven? No, you will be brought down to Hades. For if the deeds of power done in you had been done in Sodom, it would have remained to this day. But I tell you that on the day of judgment it will be more tolerable for the land of Sodom than for you" [Matt. 11:21-24].

He who utters these terrible words must know the judgment of God well. Just like the one who delivered the Beatitudes. Just like the one who came to shatter the human character of human relationships, placing himself at the interior of these relations as their very life, thus making them possible. Just as in the words already cited whose mystery begins to clear for us: "Whoever comes to me and does not hate father and mother, wife and children, brothers and sisters, yes, *and even life itself,* cannot be my disciple" (Luke 14:26; emphasis mine). For what can I prefer to my own life if not this Life which is in it and which gives it to itself, making me a living being? Yet this last question, which sanctions the ruin of any conceivable humanism, applies equally to the numerous maxims in the Gospels which seem to have only an ethical meaning. Who can actually direct to humans the new commandment to love one's enemies? Must humans not be abruptly changed at their very core, so that dismissing this self seized by hatred, they would unexpectedly give way to love, thereby ceasing to have enemies? But who brings the change about?

When, relinquishing the rules of the world, human relationship collapses in paradox, the reply is given: "The greatest among you must become like the youngest, and the leader like one who serves. For who is greater, the one who is at the table or the one who serves? Is it not the one at the table? But I am among you as one who serves" (Luke 22:26-27). Once again, this is not a mere edifying example or a model of conduct. Christ who intervenes in human relationship is not actually one of its members — neither the one who commands, nor the one who serves. He is the Word [*Verbe*] hidden in the life of each one of those on whom he confers the status of son as he delivers them. From then on, none of them belong to the human relationship, nor define themselves by the place they occupy on the stage of the world. Having never been a functionary with a position in the social order, he would not know to claim for himself any of the prerogatives that this order bestows. At the heart of the status of son, one alone operates, he in whom the gift of life accomplishes itself: "And I am among you as one who serves."

Hence the injunction does not have as its object to rectify a social structure; it is directed against the world. Having assumed the appearance of one who, poorer here than the foxes and the birds, has no place on earth at his disposal, it is nonetheless the Word [*Verbe*] of God who conceals himself from view under this absolute destitution. Who, in fact, can assign to humans a different destiny than that of the world? To the one to whom he has just said "Follow me," Christ declares in an abrupt fashion that in order to do so one must abandon earthly goals and concerns. The man answers: "Let me first go and bury my father." "But Jesus said to him, 'Let the dead bury their own dead; but as for you, go and proclaim the kingdom of God.' Another said, 'I will follow you, Lord; but let me first say farewell to those at my home.' Jesus said to him: 'No one who puts a hand to the plow and looks back is fit for the kingdom of God'" (Luke 9:57-62).

If, leaving aside these extraordinary propositions — which in each instance mean the end for the order of the world — we go back to the statements where Christ's inconceivable revelation of his divine status is achieved directly or in a thinly veiled manner, we actually find them scattered across all of the Gospels. Today, in societies which move progressively away from the rule of law, and where there is no longer either law or respect for or observance of laws, we can measure only with difficulty the import of the critique of the law in an essentially religious world whose religion is precisely that of the Law. Calling this law into question means necessarily to call into question the entire society and the foundation on which it rests. This explains the gravity of the question sometimes asked by the Pharisees and sometimes by Christ himself: "And they asked him, 'Is it lawful to cure on the sabbath?' so that they might accuse him" (Matt. 12:10). "And he said to them: 'Is it lawful to do good on the sabbath or to do evil, to save a life or to kill?' And they were silent." In the immediate context, it is a matter of a man whose right hand had been paralyzed and whom Christ heals — to the great indignation of the Pharisees. After leaving the synagogue and, after some hesitation, they decide to get rid of him. Not being able to prosecute him before the high priest, they ask Herod's people whether Herod could imprison him like John.

Another episode also recounted in the three Synoptic Gospels raises the same issue: "At that time Jesus went through the grainfields on the sabbath; his disciples were hungry, and they begun to pluck heads of grain and to eat. When the Pharisees saw it, they said to him, 'Look, your disciples are doing what is not lawful to do on the sabbath'" (Matt. 12:1-3). Christ will reply that when David and his companions were hungry, they ate the bread of the offering, which was only permitted to the priests. And that, besides, the priests themselves break the sabbath rest without committing any fault. It is in this context that assertions unbearable to the Jewish world become explosive: not content to shatter the foundation of this world, they redound on Christ in order to put him beyond the reach of any known religious criterion — beyond sinners, the just, the Law. So much do these statements identify their author with the one who holds divine power that he is identified purely and simply with it: "I tell you, *something greater than the temple is here.* But if you had known what this means, 'I desire mercy and not sacrifice,' you would not have condemned the guiltless. For *the Son of Man is lord of the sabbath*" (Matt. 12:6-8; emphasis mine).

More than the Temple, the Law, and the Sabbath. But also "greater than Jonah," "greater than Solomon." This is the charge directed by Christ against the evil generation which asks for a sign: "The queen of the South will rise at the judgment with the people of this generation and condemn them, because she came from the ends of the earth to listen to the wisdom of Solomon, and see, something greater than Solomon is here! The people of Nineveh will rise up at the judgment with this generation and condemn it, because they repented at the proclamation of Jonah, and see, something greater than Jonah is here" (Luke 11:29-32 and Matt. 12:41-42).

Consequently, how can we avoid the question that Christ asks his disciples about himself in the three Synoptics? Here is Matthew's version

(16:13-20): "Now when Jesus came into the district of Caesarea Philippi, he asked his disciples, 'Who do people say that the Son of Man is?' And they said, 'Some say John the Baptist, but others Elijah, and still others Jeremiah or one of the prophets.' He said to them, 'But who do you say that I am?' Simon Peter answered, 'You are the Messiah, the Son of the living God.' . . . Then he sternly ordered the disciples not to tell anyone that he was the Christ" (cf. Luke 9:18-21; Mark 8:27-30).

We are thus referred to the final statements Christ will formulate about his status at the time of his trial. In accordance with the consent already mentioned, Christ is first led before the Sanhedrin: "Now the chief priests and the whole council were looking for false testimony against Jesus so that they might put him to death, but they found none, though many false witnesses came forward. At last two came forward and said: 'This fellow said, "I am able to destroy the temple of God and to build it in three days."' The high priest stood up and said, 'Have you no answer? What is it that they testify against you?' But Jesus was silent. Then the high priest said to him, 'I put you under oath before the living God, tell us if you are the Messiah, the Son of God.' Jesus said to him, 'You have said so'" (Matt. 26:59-64; Mark 14:55-62; Luke 22:66-70). Thus the blasphemy was pronounced that merited death in the eyes of the Sanhedrin. As the Sandhedrin did not have the right to pronounce a death sentence, even for a religious crime, Christ was led before Pilate who in turn questioned him: "Now Jesus stood before the governor; and the governor asked him, 'Are you the King of the Jews?' Jesus said, 'You say so'" [Matt. 27:11].

Among all the words that Christ asserts about himself, the statement that he is the Christ, that is to say the Messiah, marks the culmination. All of the Gospels recount it without change in the same dramatic context. The meaning leaves no room for doubt: it has the same meaning for him who says it as for those who hear it. Jesus' identification with the Christ and the Messiah is his identification as Son of God, and his identification as Son of God is his identification with God himself. This radical claim is at issue in the trial. Despite its enormity, it is not Christ's assertion related by the final witnesses (of which, besides, they do not understand the meaning) that is upheld: "This fellow said, 'I am able to destroy the temple of God and to build it in three days.'" At stake is rather what it implies in the eyes of all, namely the identification of its author with the divine omnipotence. The high priest immediately leaps to this identification. Christ is ordered to defend himself against it. The intent of the accusation is hence the same in the eyes of the tribunal as in those of the accused. And although formulated in indirect fashion and still veiled, Christ's response has the same meaning for him as for those who will condemn him: thus its extraordinary importance.

If "the facts" and their meaning escape any dispute or ambiguity, one question at least is still asked by today's reader as it has been habitually, from generation to generation over two millennia: can the extraordinary identification of Jesus with Christ and hence with God himself receive any sort of justification? Beyond its so categorical affirmation, is Christ in a position to legitimize it? Put otherwise: does the word he speaks to humans concerning himself and in which he designates himself as Christ and the Savior of the world have any credibility?

Two paths open themselves before anyone who takes this question seriously. We have already pursued the first. We have seen how the word addressed to humans concerning themselves reverses the natural relations that they maintain spontaneously among themselves with the command directed at them to love their enemies — and how such a reversal follows from that of the human condition. It is because it can no longer be grasped according to a natural genealogy but a divine one that all that concerns humans — their actions as well as their emotions — must proceed from the origin from which they themselves derive, from their relationship with God.

On the one hand, the effects of the new definition of the human condition which starts from its divine generation appear perplexing to the eyes of the world — even destructive, to the extent that the world is no longer the ground of that definition. What do the connections between humans, if they no longer come from their nature, understood as an autonomous and social nature, mean? What is the origin of their activity if all the goals they pursue in the world are deprived of worth? One is here really assisting a collapse of the "human system."

And is this not precisely what has happened? Do we not see the catastrophe resulting not from hearing the word of Christ but from forgetting it — indeed, in today's world, from the restriction that bans it? Any sacred basis having been removed from human nature, as from the world which relies on it, humans find themselves delivered up to the facticity of material nature, to a network of blind processes devoid of any interior justification. The reciprocity of natural relationships is no longer that of love but rather, as we have seen, of rivalry, of struggle for material goods, money, power, prestige — hence the reign of artifice, of treachery, untruthfulness, adultery, envy, hatred, and violence — and finally the struggle of all against all tempered by the formation of cliques outside which the individual cannot survive any longer in the jungle of modernity. This is what happens when Christ's paradoxical word, to love those who do evil to you, loses its power. It alone can prevent the vicious cycle of vengeance and hatred. In this way the truth of Christ's word addressed to humans about themselves is inevitably realized as soon as that word is understood in its truth: "I leave you my peace, I give you my peace." Human experience emerges then as the proof of this truth. Starting from this paradoxical correspondence, since it rests on a series of paradoxes, between the word of Christ and our experience, it is possible to conceive a sort of apologetics of Christianity in the manner of Pascal.

Nevertheless, the truth of Christ's word about humans results from, and utterly depends on, the truth of Christ's word about himself. In this way one is sent back to the second path. It is the truth of the word of Christ, his identification of himself as the Son and hence with God himself, which comes into question. With regard to this truth, in and of itself, it is a matter of knowing: can it be legitimated — how and by whom?

CHAPTER 6

The Question of the Legitimacy of the Words Spoken by Christ about Himself

We have noted the repeated and more and more categorical occurrences, in which Jesus affirms that he is the Christ, the Son of God and thus God himself. Is this merely an affirmation? Is Christ, if he is the Christ, not constrained to legitimize it and to justify the truth of what he claims to be? For the question "What do you say about yourself?" is inevitably coupled with a second one: "By what right do you say that?"

And that is really the objection which will arise on numerous occasions in the synagogues where he teaches. It arises each time the content of this teaching reflects back on the one who professes it, making him, in some manner or other, directly or implicitly, *someone who is more than human, someone who is no longer only a human.*

There is thus an inevitable confrontation. And the confrontation comes in two stages. Initially, his listeners are divided. Grasping in his remarks and his actions whatever is strange or contrary to the religious law of which they are the guardians, the scribes, Pharisees, priests, and high priests readily detect the hidden affirmation from which they derive. Others, in general simpler people, who are fascinated by his words and by the authority of his person, follow him and become his disciples. Running wherever rumor announces his coming, they escort him from village to village. Or sometimes, through an encounter or the performance of a miracle, a way is opened to them to follow where he leads. Multiple clashes are thus predictable among those who want to recognize Jesus as the Christ and those who, refusing him this recognition, take him for a blasphemer. Whatever the occasion in which these conflicts explode, the true cause for their violence is always the same, namely the status of him who acts as if he is the Messiah.

Let us consider the sequence which, in the Gospel of John, follows the healing of the man blind from birth (John 9:8-34). "The neighbors and those who had seen him before as a beggar began to ask, 'Is this not the man who used to sit and beg?' Some were saying, 'It is he.' Others were saying, 'No, but it is someone like him.' He kept saying, 'I am the man.' But they kept asking him, 'Then how were your eyes opened?' He answered, 'The man called Jesus made mud, spread it on my eyes, and said to me, "Go to Siloam and wash." Then I went and washed and received my sight.'"

As in every other instance when a similar event occurs, the Pharisees investigate, calling his status into question, having placed him under close surveillance: "They brought to the Pharisees the man who had formerly been blind. Now it was on a sabbath day when Jesus made the mud and opened his eyes. . . . Some of the Pharisees said, 'This man is not from God, for he does not observe the sabbath.' But others said, 'How can a man who is a sinner perform such signs?' And they were divided. . . . The Jews did not believe that he had been blind and had received his sight until they called the parents of the man who had received his sight."

We know how the parents, for fear of being expelled from the synagogue, direct the investigators back to their son, under the pretext that he is capable of responding to them for himself. "They said to him, 'What did he do to you? How did he open your eyes?' He answered them, 'I have told you already, and you would not listen. Why do you want to hear it again? Do you also want to become his disciples?' Then they reviled him, saying, 'You are his disciple, but we are disciples of Moses. We know that God has spoken to Moses, but as for this man, we do not know where he comes from.' The man answered, 'Here is an astonishing thing! You do not know where he comes from, and yet he opened my eyes. . . . Never since the world began has it been heard that anyone opened the eyes of a person born blind. If this man were not from God, he could do nothing.' They answered him, 'You were born entirely in sins, and are you trying to teach us?' And they drove him out."

The tension between the Pharisees and the disciples — in this case concerning the blind beggar — is therefore the result of a more original conflict, the one which opposes the Pharisees to Christ himself. And the cause of the conflict, obscured by the extraordinary events which have taken place, is the status of him who, once again, places himself above the Law and the religious system developed from it. The question raised by the blasphemous character of his acts, as well as his words, is really that of their legitimacy.

This crucial question of legitimacy occurs in the three Synoptic Gospels in similar terms. "When he entered the temple, the chief priests and the elders of the people came to him as he was teaching, and said, 'By what authority are you doing these things, and who gave you this authority?' Jesus said to them, 'I will also ask you one question; if you tell me the answer, then I will also tell you by what authority I do these things. Did the baptism of John come from heaven, or was it of human origin?' And they argued with one another, 'If we say, "From heaven," he will say to us, "Why then did you not believe him?" But if we say, "Of human origin," we are afraid of the crowd; for all regard John as a prophet.' So they answered Jesus, 'We do not know.' And he said to them, 'Neither will I tell you by what authority I am doing these things'" (Matt. 21:23-27; cf. Mark 11:27-33; Luke 20:1-8).

What is going on here is far from a simple evasion — not without humor — of an annoying question. While Jesus upholds his authority intact by protecting the very profound mystery of his origin, he discredits that of his interlocutors who are constrained to admit their ignorance. It is this same reversal of authority which is operative in the famous episode of the adulterous woman, even if Christ's status does not seem to be at stake there. When the scribes and the Pharisees again want to trap him through their Law, it is well-known how Christ turns the tables on them. "Teacher, this woman was caught in the very act of committing adultery. Now in the law Moses commanded us to stone such women. Now what do you say?" While he traces signs of the ancient Law and others, unknown to them, of the new Law on the ground, the scathing reply blazes forth which still resonates today in our world deprived of sense: "'Let anyone among you who is without sin be the first to throw a stone at her.' . . . When they heard it, they went away, one by one, beginning with the elders; and Jesus was left alone with the woman standing before him. . . . 'Woman, where are they? Has no one condemned you?'" (John 8:3-11).

Where are they? No one? In the void left by this retreat, which means no less than the collapse of their supposed knowledge and that of the ethical Law with it, a sort of transfiguration occurs. The figure of Christ is wreathed in a power no man holds. In forgiving sin, he causes that which is or has been to be no longer — the hidden aspect of which is the power of causing that which is no longer, to be, to make the dead alive.

The confrontation with the Pharisees assumes not only the subtle form in which Christ's status is still only implied. Veiled in a parable, rending the world's night like a terrifying flash, comes the prophecy about God's murder by humans. Is it by chance that in the three Synoptic Gospels this parable follows immediately upon the confrontation with the Pharisees on the subject of whether Christ has the right to do what he does?

"There was a landowner who planted a vineyard. . . . He leased it to tenants. . . . When the harvest time had come, he sent his slaves to the tenants to collect his produce. But the tenants seized his slaves and beat one, killed another, and stoned another. Again he sent other slaves, more than the first; and they treated them in the same way. Finally he sent his son to them, saying, 'They will respect my son.' But when the tenants saw the son, they said to themselves, 'This is the heir; come, *let us kill him and get his inheritance*'" (Matt. 21:33-40; cf. Mark 12:1-9; Luke 20:9-16; emphasis mine). Hence the murder of the heir is accomplished, which gives the murderers the possession of the world. And in the accomplishment of that murder, humanism is born in which humans make the world and themselves their own possession, manipulating everything, including themselves, according to multiple possibilities offered to them in the world and within themselves.

But there are consequences of the murder that the end of the parable prophesies. When Christ asks what the Master will do with the tenants when he will return, the people answer: "'He will put those wretches to a miserable death, and lease the vineyard to other tenants who will give him the produce at the harvest time.' Jesus said to them, 'Have you never read in the scriptures: "The stone that the builders rejected has become the cornerstone . . . ?" Therefore I tell you, the kingdom of God will be taken away from you and given to a people that produce the fruits of the kingdom. The one who falls on this stone will be broken to pieces; and it

will crush anyone on whom it falls.' When the chief priests and the Pharisees heard his parables, they realized that he was speaking about them.
They wanted to arrest him, but they feared the crowds" (Matt. 21:41-44).

The affirmation of Christ's status as Son is thus becoming increasingly clear in his teaching. He himself now provokes the question of
knowing who he is. This time, the question is not posed to his disciples
but to those who want to ruin him. The decisive episode is likewise reported in the three Synoptic Gospels. "Now while the Pharisees were
gathered together, Jesus asked them this question: 'What do you think of
the Messiah? Whose son is he?' They said to him, 'The son of David.' He
said to them, 'How is it then that David by the Spirit calls him Lord, saying, "The Lord said to my Lord, 'Sit at my right hand, until I put your enemies under your feet'"? If David thus calls him Lord, how can he be his
son?' No one was able to give him an answer, nor from that day did anyone dare ask him any more questions" (Matt. 22:41-46; cf. Mark 12:35-37;
Luke 20:41-44).

That no one dared to question Christ on that particular day does
not mean that his affirmation of his status as Lord, that is to say, as God,
keeps people from returning to the problem of his legitimacy. We have
seen how this occurs in the Synoptic Gospels. It is in John (obviously he
also records the discussions which took place in the Temple) that the
question of Christ's legitimation of his divine status gives rise to more
intricate developments until finally it is given a reply of unfathomable
depth. For John is not content with reproducing the confrontations
which will lead to Jesus' condemnation and torment in all their tragic
tension. His plan, at first glance unrealizable, is to validate Christ's affirmation of his status as Son by placing himself as it were at the interior
of this affirmation and in being coextensive with its movement. More
radically: by placing himself at the interior of the very position of being
the Christ and in identifying with it. We will see how, far from being
foolish, this identification carries the word of Christ to the place of its
accomplishment.

We are still not in a position to comprehend these final truths. And
this is because we are incapable of understanding *what sort of comprehension* is capable of opening us to it. To say this in other words: the
propositions taken from John's Gospel on which we will reflect now are

formulated in a language which is the language of humans, the one humans speak amongst themselves, in which are written all the texts we know, especially the Gospels. It is in this language, as we have underlined, that Christ spoke to humans, inasmuch as he spoke to them as a human being. Let me point out immediately that *this human language is not the language of God*. Yet according to John, Christ is none other than the Word [*Verbe*] of God, that is to say his Word [*Parole*]. It is only when we come to know the nature of this Word [*Parole*] that we will be in a position truly to grasp what it says to us — what it says through the language that humans speak or which, for the moment, seems to us as such. So, in the brief remarks that follow and which are concerned with the text, we have only a first step. The full justification of Christ's divine status will only be able to come from God's word [*parole*] itself, lived in its original truth. It can only come from the Word [*Verbe*].

Who then could really legitimate the extraordinary affirmation by which Christ identifies himself with the Word [*Verbe*]? Or, to take up the language of his adversaries, repeated and assumed by Christ himself, what witness could stand surety for such an assertion? That is the requirement formulated by the Law. If "no one can render testimony to himself," how could Jesus evade this inescapable obligation as it concerns his extravagant pretense to make himself God?

Let me point out that, from the philosophical point of view, the reasoning of those who refer to the Law in this way is circular. In fact, the Law is addressed to humans.[1] *Thus, if Christ is a human being* — but that is exactly what is at stake in the debate — he is subject to it. Is Jesus not a human being? "You, though only a human being, are making yourself God" (John 10:33). The keepers of the Law ceaselessly assert an identity like that of everyone else, an identity defined by place of birth and by parents, in opposition to Christ's positing of his identification with the Word

1. This is the reason why this law, at root religious, will be taken up, at least in regard to the principle here in question, by all the civil codes on earth. This principle is very simple and is read easily in the following example. If I am suspected of a crime in Saumur and I declare that on that particular day, I was in Paris, my declaration is without value as long as it is not confirmed by the testimony of another human who has seen me on that particular day, at that hour, in Paris. It is this juridical law concerning human affairs that the examiners attempt to put forward against Christ's declarations about himself.

[*Verbe*]. "Yet we know where this man is from; but when the Messiah comes, no one will know where he is from" (John 7:27). For the Law only applies to a human being, as defined by an identity that finds its criteria in the world of humans: date and place of birth, name and profession of parents, etc. Such a human is not authorized to bear testimony to himself. The Pharisees are speaking to the man Jesus when they say: "You are testifying on your own behalf; your testimony is not valid" (John 8:13).

Christ's initial response seems to concede the two points of their objection to his accusers: that he is a human and that consequently, in conformity with the Law, he would not be able to testify on his own behalf: "You know me and you know where I am from." "If I testify about myself, my testimony is not true" [John 7:28; 5:31[2]]. But this initial response is obviously only a ruse. How can we fail to see that it is contrary to the teaching that Christ has ceaselessly addressed to humans *in regard to themselves?* "Do not give the name of father to anyone." Hence when the priests, the scribes, the Pharisees and their disciples believe it timely to remind him that he is the son of the carpenter Joseph and of Mary, this common belief in a natural genealogy of humans runs counter to Christ's repeated affirmation of their divine genealogy. It cannot be applied to him, even considered as a man, as a son among all the other sons. Even less does it apply to him if he is uniquely the Firstborn Son, identical to the Word [*Verbe*].

It is precisely this identity as the Firstborn Son which leads Christ to reject his subjection to the human condition, disqualifying from the outset the objection of all of them that his magical word will somehow strip them of an authority that they never held from themselves and they sense is about to escape them. The human condition is something, moreover, about which they are completely mistaken, incapable as they are of understanding the human otherwise than according to the world and its properties: space, time, causality, etc., as we would say today. Expressed in an interrogative tone — "You know me? You know who I am?" — Jesus' propositions convey their opposite: you imagine that you know me, you believe you know who I am but you know nothing of me. You quite precisely do not know from where I come; you do not know my Father.

2. [Henry translates the latter as "If I testify about myself, my testimony is without value."]

These are the dazzling declarations by which Christ, not content to reaffirm his divine status unequivocally, gives in each instance some sort of absolute justification for this exorbitant claim. "You know me and you know where I am from. I have not come on my own. But the one who sent me is true, and you do not know him. I know him, because I am from him, and he sent me." And several verses further: "I will be with you a little while longer, and then I am going to him who sent me. You will search for me, but you will not find me; and where I am, you cannot come" (John 7:28-29, 33-34).

The legalistic objection concerning testimony is thus left in tatters. In one sense, Christ has received many testimonies. Those of the Scriptures: "It is they that testify on my behalf." That of Moses: "If you believed Moses, you would believe me, for he wrote about me." And finally, that of the Baptist, in whom also they did not believe. Nevertheless, it is not from these testimonies, as important as they may be, notably that of the Baptist, that Christ awaits the final justification of his word. "I do not accept such human testimony" (respectively John 5:39; 5:46; 5:33-35; 8:14-18). Then follows a severe critique of all human testimony inasmuch as it occurs in the truth of the world, in what John calls its "light" or its "glory." It is always possible to see, to hear, to ask someone to repeat what he has said. According to the teaching of Christ already analyzed, any human action considered in regard to the appearance it offers of itself in the exteriority of the world carries within it the possibility of pretence and untruthfulness — the act of testifying, as of fasting, giving alms, or praying. Here on earth, any testimony is potentially a false testimony. It is this deficiency specific to any human word that the Law attempts to surmount in requiring the plurality of testimonies. It is this same deficiency which leads Christ to refuse any human testimony on his own behalf.[3]

---

3. There is a deeper reason for this critique: How could Christ, if he is the Word [*Parole*] of God, really be subject to the precariousness of a human word [*parole*]? It requires all the presumption, the superficiality, and the blindness of humanism for one of its patent representatives to dare to declare: "It is always I who will decide whether the voice is the voice of an angel." How could living beings, always already given to themselves in life, never hearing anything other than this Word of Life, really judge, authenticate or denigrate a Voice which always precedes them, they whose very existence is always only that of listeners? But these remarks are premature.

If Christ then does not expect testimony regarding his status from any human being, from whom can this testimony come? From himself. In the eyes of the keepers of the Law, that means to go back to a testimony without value. Yet, as we have said, Christ seems to conform to the requirement of the Law in a merely superficial fashion — not in order to accept that he is really subject to it, but in order to affirm in a new clash that he does not fall under it, situating himself infinitely above it, in the highest, the place from which he comes. Nor is Christ alone in giving testimony to his status as one sent by God; *he who has sent him testifies for him,* with him, with whom he is at one. From there come new apostrophes which gleam like the cutting edge of a sword: "If I testify about myself, my testimony is not true. There is another who testifies on my behalf, and I know that his testimony to me is true" (John 5:31-32). Who is this "other"? "And the Father who sent me has himself testified on my behalf. You have never heard his voice or seen his form, and you do not have his word abiding in you, because you do not believe him whom he has sent" (John 5:37-38).

And again: "Even if I testify on my own behalf, my testimony is valid because I know where I have come from and where I am going, but you do not know where I come from or where I am going. You judge by human standards; I judge no one. Yet even if I do judge, my judgment is valid; for it is not I alone who judge, but I and the Father who sent me. *In your law* it is written that the testimony of two witnesses is valid. I testify on my own behalf, and the Father who sent me testifies on my behalf" ([John 8:14-18], emphasis mine).

It is then the Pharisees — scandalized, but really at a loss — who are driven to blasphemy, to the negation of God. For in Christ's rejection of any human genealogy concerning him, it is really the question of the one and only Father of all humans that is raised — of this true Father who is God himself. This is the Father of whom Christ declares himself heir, of whom simultaneously he claims knowledge and testimony and of whom the Pharisees apparently do not know anything. The Pharisees said to him: "Where is your Father?" Jesus responded: "You know neither me nor my Father. If you knew me, you would know my Father also" (John 8:19).

We must now strive to clarify these impenetrable words, which contain in themselves the justification of Christ's affirmation of his divine status. And one can do so in two ways. One can attempt to grasp their radical meaning within their Johannine context, from other definitive words of Christ. A second path is open to us if we remember one of our initial remarks, one to which we have alluded on several occasions in our analysis. If Christ has two natures, we said, one human, the other divine, must he not also have two kinds of words [*paroles*], one particular to humans, the other divine, which belongs to him inasmuch as he is the Word [*Verbe*] of God: the word [*parole*] of God himself? Does the final meaning of the definitive words of Christ *not reside in his word* [parole] *inasmuch as it is that of the Word* [Verbe] *of God?* Yet in what does this word consist? The time has come for us to raise this decisive question.

CHAPTER 7

Word of the World, Word of Life

We are in the presence of a question which we have just described as decisive despite the fact that, paradoxically, it has never been posed by philosophy. If this question assumes the importance that we sense in it, it would be advisable to make this observation: taking into consideration certain fundamental religious themes permits us to discover an immense domain unknown to rational thought. Far from being opposed to a truly free reflection, Christianity would force traditional philosophy and its canonical corpus to face up to their limits, if not to say to their blindness.

At stake is finding out whether a different word exists than the one humans ordinarily speak to communicate with each other. The necessity to go back over this question of the human word, of which certain characteristics have here been briefly called to mind, is now imposed on us: Do the Scriptures not, in fact, make use of this word even when they endeavor to transmit to us the divine revelation contained therein?

It is doubtless advisable to distinguish two kinds of words in the texts of the New Testament. On the one hand, those of the evangelists, Matthew, Mark, John, and Luke, who relate the events linked to the historical existence of Christ. These events, although chosen from many others whose account has not reached us; all reveal themselves to be extremely significant, on more than one account. They mark the stages of Christ's progressive unveiling of his mission: his choice of disciples, signs of the mission, the status of him who will accomplish it, the welcome received in the regions traversed, debates in the synagogues and in the Temple, etc. Yet unlike these events, which compose the basic framework of the story, other passages stand out irresistibly. In actual fact we no longer listen to a story of Christ's feats and exploits, related by others, by witnesses. Christ himself speaks; we hear his very words. Accordingly, the text is constantly interrupted by quotation marks. The continuity of a history that everyone can follow because it develops in a familiar universe literally explodes with the irruption of these disconcerting remarks — never before heard, perhaps impossible to hear.

Yet these remarks, as strange as they may be, whether they concern the human condition or that of Christ himself, are always formulated in only one language, precisely the one which humans speak and which is also that of the Scriptures. Considered in their context, absorbed in it, similar to other propositions which compose the narration in which they are inscribed, the words of Christ have become again what they have never ceased to be, "human" words, in the sense that they are expressed in a common language. They inevitably take their forms and their structures from the nature of human language.

I have described this language as a *language of the world* and that for two reasons. On the one hand, it is a language which points to the things of the world, whether the inert things of nature, animals, or even cultural objects, the latter considered in the largest sense: they are all the objects which have some relationship with humans, which imply their intervention. It is thus that a fishing boat points to the existence of its owner or of the person who uses it as well as to those who have constructed it. A field, a vineyard, cannot be perceived without the potential representation of wheat and of bread, of grapes and of wine, of those who will consume the fruits of the earth, and of the farmers and the winegrowers who have produced them. The "human world" is composed of realities of this sort, material in a sense, but which would not be conceivable without the human beings whose needs and tasks they make visible. The animals themselves, inasmuch as they are domestic animals, are part of this human world of which they have been essential components during the course of history. In the Gospels, the words of Christ spoken to humans about their condition are full of allusions to these concrete realities from which daily existence cannot be separated. "Which one among you, if his ox . . . falls into a well on the sabbath, does not immediately pull it out?"[1]

Yet here is the second reason why we call the language which serves to designate the multiple realities of our environment a "language of the world." Whatever these realities may be, we can really speak of them only if they show themselves to us. And this is true not only for these realities themselves but for the group of qualities that we are led to attribute to them in the course of our immediate perception or in the judgments that we form regarding them.

Therefore the question is raised: how do they show themselves to us? In the philosophical tradition from which modernity arises, the reply is demanded from the most ordinary experience: the things — stones, flowers, earth and sky, the products of the earth, tools and machines, humans themselves — all these realities show themselves to us in the world. Consequently, the widespread belief takes birth which defines what is called "common sense" and according to which *the world is the environment of all possible manifestation.* In other words: the universe of the visible is the only world which exists; it defines the ground of reality.

Now, if we can only speak of what shows itself to us, and if all that shows itself to us does so in the world, then any word is linked to the world by an insuperable link. *We can only speak of what shows itself to us in the world.* This does not mean only sensible objects, like stones, mountains, trees, houses, fields, factories or even human beings — all things that we can see with our eyes, or of which we can perceive the qualities, the smells, the sounds with all of our senses. "Intelligible" and insensible

---

1. Previously cited, this verse is interesting in many respects, "overdetermined" as are almost all the words of Christ, of which the analysis discovers new meanings each time. This word does not only illustrate the concrete character of the examples to which Christ has recourse; it does not only go back to a general critique of legalism. Being opposed directly to a proposition of the Master of Justice, it permits us to refute the thesis according to which Christianity is only a version of an Essene community, "an Essenism which has succeeded." The indisputable reference to the Gospel situation of the Baptist, like the Baptist and Christ himself in the "desert," that is to say in the community of Qumran, only serves to underline the entire originality of Christianity and of the New Alliance which it came to bring to the world of Judaism. One knows that the spirituality of Qumran awaited the perfection of a strict observance of the Law, for which Christ substituted a completely different Law, the Commandment of Love.

things, like geometrical properties, mathematical or logical relations, must equally be added here: we "see" them also with the eyes of our mind; we can comprehend them in a series of "evidences." This means that thanks to a process of distancing they hold themselves in the same manner *before* our mind, in the exteriority of the "world." It is in the light of this exteriority that they show themselves to us, so that we can actually describe them, analyze them, *and before that, name them, speak of them.*

"Word of the world" hence means: a word which speaks of what shows itself to us in this exteriority that is the world. It is thus that, in a concrete manner, "appearing" is put forward as the condition of possibility of any word, to the point that we can only speak of what shows itself to us. This appearing, the condition that makes the word possible, is nothing other than what the Greeks called the Logos. Yet if the word finds its possibility in appearing, then must not the properties of this word likewise depend on this appearing? And if this appearing is the appearing of the world, that is to say this process of distancing, this exteriority in the light of which we see everything about which we can speak, do the properties of the word of the world then not necessarily depend on the properties of the world itself?

That is the case. Let me present briefly three essential traits which belong to the appearing in the world. First because this appearing is a milieu of pure exteriority, all that shows itself and becomes visible in it shows itself as exterior, as other [*autre*] than us, as different from us. Such is the case with the totality of objects — sensible or intelligible — which compose the visible universe.

Second, the appearing of the world does not refer only to what is exterior, other, different from everything that is shown in it. It is at the same time totally indifferent to it. It matters little whether its light illuminates the empty bed of a wadi or an abundant river, a fertile field or desolate earth, a friendly gathering or a bloody battle. On the world's stage, on the scene of history appear alternately beings full of grace or monsters, charitable acts or genocides, monasteries devoted to meditation with their precious libraries, the fires which destroy them, invasions which annihilate cities, irreplaceable civilizations and cultures. All this shows itself to us in the same way, in a terrifying neutrality. They are facts, and in their objectivity — this objectivity of which modernity and its sciences are so proud — all these facts are equivalent.

Finally, the third trait. The appearing of the world is indifferent to all that it shows for a most profound reason: because it is incapable of positing its existence, of creating it. Reduced to its exteriority, the world is only an empty environment, a horizon devoid of content. The making-seen — which makes visible all things in the light of this pure empty milieu — in no way determines what it encounters. Like a traveler leaning out of the window of a train, it is limited to what flashes past under its powerless gaze.

Such are the characteristics that the word takes from the appearing of the world. Because this latter is an environment of pure exteriority where everything shows itself as external, other, or different, the word of the world — which speaks of what it sees in it — speaks necessarily of something other than it, external to it, different from it, to which it is totally indifferent, and over which it has no power.

If we consider the theories of language which have played such a great role in modern thought, we see that, whether consciously or not, they have only applied to language properties which follow directly from the foundation that they assign to it, in order to know this appearing of the world, the visible universe with which common sense identifies all reality. The most obvious of all these properties is *the referential character of language.* From it one understands that all language, any term, refers to a content external to it and different from it. In this way *the term is not the reality which it designates,* that is to say, it is limited to making it seen. The term "dog" refers to the real dog, but it is in itself, as a term, no real dog. It refers or signifies it "emptily." The word is an "empty signification." This incapacity of the term to produce the reality which it designates is the most general characteristic of language that is at stake here. Saying "I have a hundred dollar bill in my pocket," does not mean I actually possess one. This is the poverty of the language humans speak and that I call, for all the reasons which I have just recounted, the "language of the world."

Reflecting further on the deficiency of these theories of language, we see that it does not consist in attributing to language properties which are not its own. Rather, it consists in considering this language to be the only one that exists. Hence these theories are fooled by the naive belief according to which the visible universe constitutes the milieu of the only true reality and consequently the only object of knowledge and language. An immense gap widens in our culture: a different word, more original and more essential than that of the world, is shown to be completely overlooked.

Let us remind ourselves here of what Christ taught us, especially concerning ourselves, us humans. What he has contended on multiple occasions and in several ways, is precisely that we are beings of this world, explicable by it, comprehensible in its terms. Undoubtedly we appear in the light of this world, in what it calls its "glory." Furthermore, always in this light, we are open to it and to all that is found in it. But the visible universe does not exhibit our true reality, which resides in the "secret" where God sees us. This is the reason why the teaching of Christ concerning the human condition has constantly substituted a divine genealogy for its worldly genealogy. According to it, the human being is a living being engendered in life, in the one and only life which exists, which is that of God. The human being is the son of God.

The problem of the word then must be examined in its relation to the living beings we are and more precisely in its relation to the Life which makes us into living beings. Life, according to our previous observations, is not a thing, a being, or a genre of a particular being, a set of phenomena specifically called "biological" and that contemporary biology reduces to material processes, insensible and without initiative. Life, life as we experience it, which is our life, is in itself a revelation — this unique form of revelation in which who reveals and what is revealed are one and the same. For this reason, I have called it a self-revelation. Such a mode only belongs to life and truly constitutes its essence. Living actually consists in this: "experiencing oneself," "being revealed to oneself." Such is the decisive and indisputable trait of the human condition, which distinguishes it irresistibly from any other.

If an essential relationship exists between the word and appearing, if a word can only speak of what is manifested to it in some fashion, an entirely new question is posed to us. To the extent that Life is a revelation, does it not at the same time make possible a word which is proper to it? To the extent that the revelation that is particular to life is the revelation of self, is not what we name this word at the same time fixed? *Revealing itself to itself, life speaks to us of itself.* We have seen that the Greeks called the possibility of the word Logos. They had situated this possibility in an appearing in which everything about which we can speak is shown to us. They had understood this appearing as the light of the world or of "nature" — as an exteriority, because it is in exteriority that an "outside" of any sensible or intelligible vision can see what presents itself to it each time as a content placed before its gaze, as an "object" or an "in front of."

With Christianity arises the incredible intuition of a different Logos — a Logos which is really a revelation. Yet it is no longer the visibility of the world, but the self-revelation of Life. This is a word whose possibility is Life itself and in which life speaks of itself, in revealing itself to itself — in which our own life is constantly spoken to us. Here John's breathtaking statements resound: "Logos of Life," "Word of Life" (1 John 1); or, in the famous Prologue of his Gospel: "In the beginning was the Word [*Verbe*] and the Word was with God and the Word was God. . . . In him was Life" (John 1:1, 4).

Before analyzing this Word of Life in a more profound fashion, which will permit us to understand all of Christ's words and especially those in which he declares himself to be this Word of Life which is that of God, that is to say his Word [*Verbe*], it is advisable to return to the essential relationship that unites the word and life. This relationship is not the object of a speculative affirmation, a theory as contestable as all theories. It is matter of an indisputable experience. How can we not recognize it at work in our own life and in each of its modalities — for example, in suffering? Suffering proves itself. That is the reason why, so we say, only suffering permits us to know suffering. *It is only in this way that suffering speaks to us; it speaks to us in its suffering. And what it says to us, by speaking to us in this way, is that it suffers, that it is suffering.* In this way a word uncovers itself to us, in its extreme simplicity, one to which the many theories of language have never paid the least attention despite their sophistication. Yet this most simple word is also the most remarkable. And its peculiarity consists in the fact that this word and what it says to us are one.

This word in which the inviolable identity of the word and of what it says to us — of the saying and the said — arrives, is not, however, limited to suffering. Any of life's modes speak to us in this manner. Joy as much as sadness, anguish, or despair; unsatisfied desire as much as effort and the feeling of fulfillment that accompanies it. That which speaks in all these tonalities which are the substance of our life — and hence is not any of them — is the omnipotent power in which each is given to itself, experiences itself, is revealed to itself, the very self-revelation of life. This is the original revelation, establishing as such an original word [*parole*], which John calls the Word [*Verbe*] of God and which is his Word [*Parole*].

We are now in a position to propose a systematic presentation of the characteristics of this Word. Just as the characteristics of the word of the world depend on the appearing of the world, so must not those of the Word of Life depend on the characteristics of Life? We have seen how, speaking of what shows itself in the exteriority of the world, the word of the world speaks of content which is external to it and which, moreover, it is incapable of creating. In its powerlessness to establish the reality about which it speaks, yet one power remains to it, namely that of affirming this reality when it does not exist: that of lying. That is the reason why, as John has suggested, the witness this word carries is potentially a false testimony. It is also why the Law required that there would always be several witnesses; according to it, one witness alone, that of Christ to himself in this instance, is devoid of value.

It is the fallacious power of the word of the world that James in his turn affirms in a startling passage in his Epistle. Because the word [*mot*] is foreign to reality and does not contain any of its properties, because it can call two different things by the same name or attribute several names to a same thing, one might as well substitute one thing for another, identify one with the other, apply an equivalent value to it, bend it to itself, reduce it to one's desire or folly. It is then that its power becomes frightening, pretending to impose its laws on reality, subjecting it to its caprice: "If we put bits into the mouths of horses to make them obey us, we guide their whole bodies. Or look at ships: though they are so large that it takes strong winds to drive them, yet they are guided by a very small rudder wherever the will of the pilot directs. . . . How great a forest is set ablaze by a small fire! And the tongue is a fire . . . a whole world of iniquity" (James 3:3-6). The continuation of the text shows how by pretending to praise the Lord while cursing humans who are made in his image, the same word blesses and curses alternatively the same reality, that of God and that of humans who are his work.

We thus recognize the decisive traits of the Word of Life, which is that of God, in their opposition to those of the word of the world, term for term. The first thing that differentiates it totally from the word of the world such as James's vivid analysis describes, is the fact that it is a word of Truth. For if the word of the world carries in it the permanent possibility of pretense and of hypocrisy, being capable of affirming what does not exist or denying what does exist, or even of blessing and cursing alternately the same reality, the Word of Life, in contrast, is incapable of lying. Its simplest and most common forms, those of the word of suffering analyzed above, witness to this.

Someone assuredly can say "I suffer" when he does not suffer, or even: "What a marvelous time!" when he feels only boredom. But it is the word of the world which speaks in that case, a word which is related to a referent external to it, to a simulated suffering, a non-existing happiness. Hence the suffering which intervenes in the proposition "I suffer" is not the "signification-suffering," an unreal representation, mental content designed by consciousness. This signification formed by the mind is only *a representation of suffering, not suffering itself.* In itself, this representative content does not suffer, any more than the concept of "dog barks." The word of the world speaks *about* suffering; it speaks of it as a reality actually external to it, different from it, to which it can moreover be completely indifferent. It declares that one must know how to accept suffering, that it belongs to the human condition, or on the contrary that it is an evil, that the many technologies science puts at our disposal will eventually succeed in eliminating it. And this discourse can be continued indefinitely without any real suffering being actually implied in it.

The word *of* suffering is completely different. It does not hold forth about suffering; it does not use any term, no spoken or written sign, no signification; it does not rely on completely unreal significations by suitable constructions of language — verbs, conjunctions, and so forth. Suffering speaks in its suffering and by it, it is one with what it says, one flesh suffering that to which it is delivered without power to escape from it or to undo it. Thus indeed the word of suffering knows nothing about duplicity; it is in itself, in the actuality of its suffering to which it testifies from itself without going back to any other testimony. It is true absolutely; its word is a word of truth.

Yet the word of suffering is in no way true by itself. It is only in the self-revelation of life that suffering is experienced and speaks to us thus of itself, in such a way that its word does not differ from what it says. The possibility of the word of suffering is contained in the Word of Life. This is why Life speaks to us in the joy of effort as much as in anguish or despair, or in whatever other tonalities we experience. These tonalities in which our existence is constantly altered are, properly speaking, only various ways in which this Life reveals itself in us and speaks to us.

The truth of each one of the tonalities, in which our existence is ceaselessly changing and about which it speak to us, is hence the Truth of Life. We recognize here an essential relationship particular to Christianity and which confers on it its extreme originality: *the relationship of Truth and Life.* It constitutes the substrate of the most primitive and the most important texts, in particular of the Gospel of John. It will be indispensable to return to it. Let me indicate now how the Truth reveals Life and belongs to it. Life is Truth because it reveals itself to itself and this revelation of itself — this self-revelation — constitutes the foundation of any conceivable truth. Nothing exists in fact for us except what manifests itself to us. Yet this presupposes that the manifestation itself manifests itself, that revelation reveals itself — as it does in this self-revelation which precisely defines the essence of Life. All these original properties that one attributes to Truth, the fact for example that Truth proves itself *(verum index sui),* that it is a self-attestation, that it is what witnesses to itself, are only manifold expressions of this self-revelation which only accomplishes itself in Life and which is its Word [*Parole*], this Word of Life which never lies.

We have already recognized how this self-revelation is accomplished in which Life speaks of itself and continues to say what it is in its truth. While the word of the world speaks of what is made manifest in the indifference of exteriority, the Word of Life speaks in a feeling, in this feeling in which it experiences itself each time, hence in a way filled with pathos. About this revelation of pathos we have learned many things. Suffering was the first thing to help us discover that Life speaks to us and that its Word has nothing to do with that of the world, the object of the sciences of language. Suffering speaks to us in itself, spurning any signification as well as written or oral signs which are its "carriers," without leaving itself, which is what one indicates in philosophy under the title of "immanence." Yet *immanence is neither a signification nor a concept, similar to those of which human language makes use.* The primitive affectivity, in which life experiences itself immediately and never in the world, is in contrast an impressional and affective reality, flesh filled with pathos. It is only because it experiences itself and reveals itself to itself in a way filled with pathos, in the immanence of this primitive affectivity, that Life is a Word [*Parole*] and a Word [*Parole*] which speaks about itself. It is only because, in turn, each of our affective tonalities is given to itself in the pathos-filled self-revelation of Life, because the Word of Life speaks in it, that we speak in turn, in the way it does, in its suffering or in its joy. All the characteristics of this word depend on characteristics of the Word of Life.

Thus it now demands our exclusive attention. And this in an urgent fashion, if it is true that this Word [*Parole*] of Life is that of God, his Word [*Verbe*]. And Christ, *inasmuch as he is the Word* [Verbe] *of God,* will legitimate that he is this Word [*Parole*] through all the unsettling words he has spoken about himself and in which he affirms being himself this Word [*Parole*] of God — his Word [*Verbe*].

CHAPTER 8

The Word of God: Self-Justification of the Words Spoken by Christ about Himself

To understand this Word [*Parole*] of Life which is the Word [*Verbe*] of God is to comprehend first *in what way Life is a word* [*parole*]. We have made important progress on this path. Recalling the profound Greek intuitions according to which any word implies the manifestation of that of which it speaks, we have indicated the prejudice that has come to jeopardize the developments of a thought that is, in itself, fertile. The manifestation implied in any word was interpreted in a unilateral fashion as that of the world. The ordinary conceptions of language, whether classical or contemporary, follow from this interpretation. According to them, language differs in principle from that about which it speaks, in such a way that it can as easily be lying as truthful, depending on whether it corresponds to the reality it pretends to express or not. Hence an entire culture will depend on two essential givens: on the one hand the intuition of a relationship between a word and the manifestation on which it depends; on the other hand, the identification of this founding manifestation of the word to the appearing of the world — to this exteriority which, among other consequences, separates the word from that which it says, the saying from its said.

If, however, a different mode of manifestation than that of the world exists, namely that of Life — a life such as ours, whose property is to reveal itself to itself — then there is also another word for which this self-revelation of life constitutes the possibility. On several occasions we have recognized how each modality of our life is a word which speaks itself — how suffering says its suffering and joy its joy — and this to the extent to which each of these tonalities experiences itself in the self-revelation of life.

Situated at the heart of reality as its original revelation, the Word of Life is the great omission of contemporary reflection, as of traditional philosophical thought. Nevertheless, it stirred up a great culture, more ancient than Greek culture and maybe more essential. This is the religious culture that we call Judeo-Christianity. What legitimates this designation — which has been contested for polemical and superficial reasons — is the extraordinary unity resulting from such a decisive situation. Whether one considers the Old or the New Testament, what is found at the center of the texts which compose them as well as in the ethics they prescribe and even more in the principle of the human condition which derives from them, is the Word [*Parole*] of God. In all cases, the human being is defined by his or her link to this Word and that in two ways: as the one to whom the word is destined and as the one whose nature it is to hear this word — even if, an unnatural and lost son, the human being no longer understands it. Also in all cases, this word is the Word [*Parole*] of Life.

Let us signal certain particularly significant occurrences of this word in the Old Testament where it appears constantly. At times, the word apparently is not addressed to anyone, resonating in some way in the void. "God said: 'Let there be light!' And there was light" (Gen. 1:3). Similar apparently to the word of humans, this word contains an essential relationship to exteriority. Nevertheless, it differs from it entirely in virtue of its creative power. In fact, it produces this exteriority, as well as everything that shows itself in it. It is by his word that God makes the world and all the things which are in it. "God said: 'Let there be a firmament. . . .' And God made the firmament" (Gen. 1:6, 7; KJV). "God said: 'Let the waters under the sky be gathered together into one place. . . .' And it was so" (Gen. 1:9).

Most often in the Old Testament, however, the words are addressed to human beings, mostly to the prophets who, from then on, utter this word of God and are recognized as doing so. The connection that links humans to God is hence made through the intermediary of other humans, who receive from their function an eminent dignity. Yet God also speaks directly to humans, to the most ordinary humans, even to murderers. "And God said to Cain: 'Where is your brother Abel?'" (Gen. 4:9). Indeed, when God speaks to humans through the prophets, it is most often to denounce their sin, predict their misfortune unless they rectify their conduct — which had become idolatrous — and attempt to lead them back to himself. That is the case with the law of Moses.

In the New Testament, the situation is totally different and Christ is not a prophet. Many of those who encounter him, impressed by his acts as well as by his words, certainly have the tendency, at first, to consider him in that manner. "Sir," said the Samaritan woman to him, "I see that you are a prophet." Yet this appearance quickly dissipates. If Christ's words, instead of being accepted like those of prophets, arouse doubt and eventually protest and rage, it is because he who professes them declares to be, himself, the Word [*Parole*] of God and thus God himself. And if these words come again into question in our analysis, it is precisely because it is they who must justify Christ's affirmation according to which he is the Word [*Verbe*] of God. From there follows the task which cannot be deferred: to grasp finally what the Word [*Verbe*] *is.*

On this crucial point, we find at our disposal, at the boundary between the two Testaments, enlightening both one and the other, the initiatory text which forms the Prologue of John's Gospel. This Prologue is not isolated. It was not an afterthought, put by chance where one encounters it, coming from who knows where. Nor is it the interpretation of a brilliant theologian, destined to make us understand what the Word [*Verbe*] of God is according to him. In reality, the Prologue constitutes the summary and conclusion of the Gospel of John. Whatever might be the date of its definitive and complete redaction, this Gospel comes, as the others, from a collection of early texts, without a doubt the most primitive. This collection was formed from a set of notes relating to Christ's words themselves heard by a disciple who accompanied the Master during the final months of his earthly existence. The redaction of these notes by "him whom Jesus loved" must have followed immediately the Passion and death of Christ. These final words of Christ are gathered in the Gospel of John of which the Prologue presents the dazzling summary. Leaving to the exegetes the concern of commenting from the linguistic or historical point of view on the series of verses of the Prologue, I will limit myself here to recalling a few of their essential affirmations.

According to the first, God is Life. That is what the analysis of Christ's words has taught us. In this way the connection of the Prologue to the direct teaching of Christ is confirmed. Let me emphasize immediately a very weighty implication of this thesis: the question of the existence of God, on which philosophy and speculative theology concentrates, is set aside. The introductory Johannine statements do not deal with this question in the least. Plunging from the outset into the hidden nature of the divinity, they tell us what it is: Life. Yet, if God is Life, two decisive consequences follow: on the one hand, we know what God is. We know it not via our thinking, according to the shaky reasons of an understanding which undertakes to reflect on God without knowing why and, trying to grasp some aspect of him, sees precisely nothing. *We know it because we are living beings and because living beings are living only if they carry Life in themselves not as a secret unknown to them but as that itself which they experience without cease, as that in which they experience themselves, as their own essence and their very reality.* If God is Life, then, as Meister Eckhart will say, the human being — this living being in the life which we each are — is "a human who knows God" *(ein Gott wissender Mensch).*[1] Furthermore, this singular affirmation is formulated by Christ on several occasions as the Gospel of John progresses: "I do not call you servants any longer, because the servant does not know what the master is doing; but I have called you friends, because I have made known to you everything that I have heard from my Father" (John 15:15). The affirmation of human knowledge of God is even stronger, restored to its radical immanence, in all the texts where Christ prophesies the unity of all those who will be in him, one with him, like he himself is one with the Father (see below, end of chapter 10).

We can nevertheless not forget a distinction that imposed itself on us in detail in our preceding reflections, namely that which separates a finite life like ours from the infinite Life which is that of God. A finite life is a life incapable of giving itself to itself, of bringing itself into the marvelous condition of being a living being. Our life is not grounded in itself. We have seen how, living from a finite life, our flesh is marked by a lack, decimated by needs and desires which perpetually recur. No water stills

1. *Treatises and Sermons,* Sermon #10.

our thirst. A yawning question arises: *How can what is in itself deprived of the power of living nevertheless live? Left to itself, a finite life is impossible. Precisely because it does not carry in itself the power to live, our life can only live in the infinite Life which does not cease to give it life.* No finite life can be separated from this all-powerful Life in which it lives: it collapses into nothingness. How does the infinite Life of God give life to all finite life, to these living beings that we are? That is a question to which I will endeavor to respond. The solution presupposes, however, that we must first answer another much more difficult inquiry, which seems to go beyond the limits of our intelligence: *How does the infinite Life, the all-powerful Life capable of bringing itself into life, accomplish in itself the eternal work of giving life to itself?* For it is only such a life, in its omnipotence, which is capable of giving, in its turn, life to all living beings.

It is to this final question that the Prologue responds. Having identified God with Life, John understands this absolute Life as the eternal movement in which it comes to itself, that is to say, engenders itself. The self-generation of Life is thus its coming in the condition which is its own, that of experiencing itself. Yet no proof is possible if the *Ipseity* in which life reveals itself to itself does not appear in it — in such a way that it becomes Life in this revelation of self, in this self-revelation. Yet absolute Life is not a concept or an abstraction: it is a real life which experiences itself really in itself. That is why the Ipseity in which it experiences itself is also an effective and real Ipseity: it is a real Self, the First Living Self in which absolute Life actually experiences itself and reveals itself to itself. Because this self-revelation is accomplished in him, this First Living Self is his Word [*Verbe*], his Word [*Parole*]. It is in this way that the eternal self-generation of Life generates its Word [*Verbe*] in itself, the "only firstborn Son" in whom it experiences itself and loves itself eternally. In the same way, the Son experiences himself and loves himself eternally in this life which engenders him in engendering itself. To say this more concisely: God engenders himself as his Word [*Verbe*]. God engenders his Word [*Verbe*] as himself. Or as John says it: "In him (in the Word [*Verbe*]) was Life (God)" (John 1:4).

The Word [*Verbe*] thus does not come at the end of the movement of absolute Life, as if it was produced by it. To the contrary, the movement by which absolute Life comes eternally into itself is accomplished in and by the generation in it of its Word [*Verbe*]. It is in him that, experiencing itself and revealing itself to itself, it is made Life. God reveals himself in his Word [*Verbe*]. The Word [*Verbe*] does not come after Life because it is in Life, in that it comes forth from itself, it reveals itself to itself, and rejoices in itself. Thus the Word [*Verbe*] is consubstantial and contemporary with Life, as ancient as it is. "In the beginning was the Word."

"In the beginning was the Word, and the Word was with God, and the Word was God. . . . In him was Life" (John 1:1-4). Let me add some indispensable details to these statements of such great depth. Being near to God means: being in God. The process of self-generation of absolute Life as generation in it of his Word [*Verbe*] is a radically immanent process. Its movement remains in itself even in its accomplishment, never goes outside of itself, never leaves itself. It is precisely because the Word [*Verbe*] meets itself in each point of its being that it does not cease to experience *itself* in this Self. It is because it constantly generates this Self that it is given to life to be this revelation of self in which the "living" of any real life consists.

An essential distinction opens up to us here between this process of generation and that of creation. Creation is the creation of the world; it consists in the opening of this horizon of exteriority, of this "Outside" where any thing becomes visible in showing itself to us outside of us — hence as external, as different, as other. Creation is always an extrinsic creation, placing what it creates outside of itself. In any form of creation — whether of artists, artisans, or industry — it is easy to recognize this structure of externalization which was and which is that of the world in its creation by God.

That life is foreign to this and to any possible exteriority, that nothing separates it from itself, that it would never be outside of itself because when, ceasing to experience itself by itself, it would cease to be life: that is what removes it from the principle of any possible creation. *Life is uncreated. Stranger to creation, stranger to the world, any process imparting Life is a process of generation.* It is an immanent process in which Life remains in the Living One whom it generates and never places itself outside itself. It is thus that in the process of self-generation of absolute Life as generation of its Word [*Verbe*] in it, Life remains in him — this Word [*Verbe*] in which it experiences itself, reveals itself to itself and rejoices in itself. Yet because in such a process where there is neither creation nor world, where nothing is placed outside of self, all remains in itself, all is immanent, one must thus say: just as Life remains in its Word [*Verbe*] in which it experiences itself, so the Word [*Verbe*] remains in this Life which it experiences in it and in which it experiences itself. Thus the Father (Life all-powerful which self-engenders itself) remains in his Son (the Word [*Verbe*] in which this Life engenders itself in experiencing itself and in revealing itself in this way to itself), just as the Son (this Son in whom Life experiences itself and loves itself infinitely) remains in this Life (which experiences itself in him in such a way that it experiences itself in it). Thus one is in the other in this way, the Father in his Son, the Son in his Father according to a reciprocal inwardness (each experiencing, living, loving one in the other), which is an interiority of love, which is their common Love, their Spirit.

We could say that, placed at the caesura of the two Testaments, John's Prologue enlightens both. One word only on the way in which it retroactively makes possible a correct reading of Genesis. This reading actually often remains quite naive. For one, such a reading considers this text as an empirical description of the origins of the human species on earth, without any relationship to everything that science can teach us today. In truth, Genesis proposes something completely different to us: *the first true and rigorous analysis of the human condition.* Instead of depending on an external presentation of facts, it goes back to the internal possibility of existence of a being that is a human. Yet, if one considers this analysis more attentively, one sees that it divides in two: *the human is here understood in two different ways, from the idea of creation but also from the idea of generation.* On the one hand, God has created the world as external to himself — the world as all the things which show themselves in their exteriority, here including the human. It is thus interpreted as contemporary objectivism still does, whether it be that of common sense or that of science: as a being-of-the-world, explainable starting from it.

How could one not see that another and totally different interpretation is superimposed on this one? According to the fundamental affirmation of Genesis (Gen. 1:26), *God made humans in his image and his likeness.* Hence, the substance from which human reality is made is the divine reality itself: *God being Life, the human is a living being.* An understanding of this implies that a completely different relationship is substituted for the extrinsic relation to the world, namely that of Life to living beings, as a relationship of immanence radically foreign to the world. It is this immanent relationship of Life to the living that the Prologue describes. It describes it in the place where it originally occurs, where absolute Life engenders itself in engendering in it the First Living Being. Even more, because this process of self-generation of Life as generation of the First Living Being is that in which life reveals itself to itself, John understands this First Living Being as him in whom absolute Life says what it is, as the Word [*Verbe*] of God, in fact, as his Word [*Parole*]. Here is why this word in which the immanent self-revelation of Life is accomplished differs in every way from all those in the world. It is not paradoxical in the least to observe one more time that it remains unknown to philosophers, linguists, and any number of exegetes.

But this is the moment for us to remember what we have also said about the Prologue: that it is the summary of the Gospel of John. The theses that it formulates are, consequently, a synthesis of numerous words of Christ of which this Gospel is the timeless memorial. On the one hand, the Prologue confirms the words in which, whether in an openly avowed or covert manner, Christ asserts that he is the Word [*Parole*] of God. On the other hand and conversely, one can say that the words of Christ recorded in this Gospel confirm the truth of the Prologue. They testify that its origin is not at all foreign to primitive Christian texts; it is neither a canticle nor a fragment of philosophy derived from elsewhere and placed by chance at the beginning of a composite whole. The evident relationship of the Prologue and the Gospel that follows it is not merely a fact of historical importance. In the circularity established between them, the truth which flows through them advances in dizzying fashion. And with it, the ability of understanding these decisive texts receives extra power.

Yet in what does this new intelligibility consist? In a simple increase of the clarity offered to our reason and demanded by it? Instead of a kind of progress, is not a change of nature at stake, a move to a radically different type of intelligibility, if it is true that the word which speaks to us is no longer that of the world? Does not the Incarnation of the Word [*Verbe*] in the flesh of Christ, according to verse 14 of the Prologue, point to him

86

who speaks in the rest of the Gospel as the Word [*Parole*] itself of Life. It is Christ himself who tells us that his Word [*Parole*] is that of God, of the God who is Life. Yet the many statements which formulate this affirmation in a variety of ways are not mere assertions. They are part of a network of implications which compose what we have called a discourse of Christ about himself and which results in *Christ's definition of himself as the One who he is.*

The first justification of the identity of the Word of Christ with that of God is based on this: Many people, on the strength of partial, provisional, or simply false evidence, speak of a myriad of things scattered around the world and in history without relation to the absolute Life of God. In contrast, Christ knows this Life, Christ knows God: "I know him, because I am from him" (John 7:29; cf. John 17:25). The reason for Christ's knowledge of God is thus immediately brought forward: it is his origin. "I came from God and now I am here" (John 8:42). The phrase "him who sent me," which always refers to God, returns without cease (cf. John 4:34; 5:24, 30; 6:29, 39, 57; 7:16, 18, etc.). Yet this origin is not the simple point of departure of an existence capable of separating from it. Heaven is the true dwelling-place of Christ. It is the place he alone knows, from where he comes, where he will return. That is because he remains in this origin in which he is consubstantial with the life of which he is the self-revelation, where he knows it, whose Word [*Parole*] he is.

In this way a series of suggestions emerges concerning the *testimony* which Christ gives and the *teaching* he delivers. Any reference to human testimony, to the necessity of a plurality of witnesses as the Law requires, is here swept aside, because it is no longer a matter of a potentially mendacious human word, but of the Word [*Parole*] of Life which witnesses to itself since it is no other than its self-attestation. In this way, the second witness demanded by the Pharisees comes forward: the Father. "The Father who sent me testifies on my behalf" (John 8:18). And because the Father is the Life which, in its self-revelation, speaks in Christ, therefore the word of Christ speaks the Truth. "The one who sent me speaks the truth and I declare to the world what I have heard from him" (8:26).

Consequently, the nature of Christ's teaching is clearly defined. "My teaching is not mine, but his who sent me" (John 8:16). "I speak these things as the Father instructed me" (John 8:28). This justifies the reason given by Christ for the relevance of the judgment which follows from this teaching. Its soundness stems from the fact that this teaching and this judgment do not proceed from a particular will but from that of God. "As I hear, I judge; and my judgment is just, because I seek to do not my own will but the will of him who sent me" (John 5:30). There is yet another proof — to which we will return at length because it concerns this time the human being itself — for the divine origin of Christ's word. And this proof will also result from the fact that Christ's teaching does not come from him but from God: "Anyone who resolves to do the will of God will know whether the teaching is from God or whether I am speaking on my own" (John 7:17; cf. below, Conclusion).

We therefore discover the complexity of the development according to which Christ identifies himself with the Word [*Parole*] of God. This is in some sense an obvious complexity, because it obeys a sort of strategy that we have already seen at work on several occasions. What Christ will say to humans is so surprising, so intolerable for them (whether they be Jews or Greeks), that he employs a detour. Instead of affirming from the outset that he *is* the Word [*Parole*] of God — of this God who, as Life and self-revelation of himself, is the original Word [*Parole*] itself — Christ brings about a sort of separation between his own word and that of God. What he says only repeats what he has heard said by God. This separation is constant in the texts we have just cited: "My teaching is not my own." "All that I speak is from the Father." "If what I say is true, it is because he has sent me," and so forth. Yet, finally, what relationship does he maintain with him who has sent him? Is it that merely of a prophet, inspired by the Spirit and different from him? What prophet would ever pretend to be God?

Yet here is an even stranger text: at the very moment where the separation between the word of Christ and that of God seems posited one more time, it is suddenly found to be abolished. Christ announces that he has not come to judge the world but to save it. The moving figure of the merciful Christ, who pardons and does not cease to forgive, arises before us. Yet, what follows is relentless: "I do not judge anyone who hears my words and does not keep them, for I did not come to judge the world. . . . The one who rejects me and does not receive my word *has a judge; on the last day the word that I have spoken will serve as judge*" (John

12:47-48). Christ's word here is no longer that of the man of mercy. It is also no longer a word learned from another and repeated; it is the Word [*Parole*] of God himself with which Christ identifies his own because it is identical to it.

The identity of the Word [*Parole*] of Christ and that of God thus reflects the identity of Christ and God himself. We know how this identity, designated most often under the title of unity, spans all the Synoptic Gospels. It is equally hammered out by John. Not only is this unity proclaimed in a repeated manner — "The Father and I are one" (John 10:30) — but John *makes clear the way in which it occurs:* in immanence, from which reciprocal interiority results, in virtue of which the Son is in the Father, who is in the Son. Yet it is not John who affirms this reciprocal interiority in what becomes an explanation or an interpretation later on. John only transmits Christ's words himself, words that we have been led to cite on several occasions. To Philip: "Do you not believe that I am in the Father and the Father is in me?" "As you, Father, are in me and I am in you" (John [14:10], 17:21). It is according to this reciprocal interiority that the unity of the Father and the Son is that which it is, not an ecstatic and abstract unity, but the violence of an original love where each one finds in the other his reality and his joy. And this is in the absence of any exteriority — let us recall this essential text: "You loved me before the foundation of the world" (17:24) — in the undivided interiority in which life is embraced. It is this enjoyment [*jouissance*] of the self in the other that the final words of Christ express. It is enjoyment that defines the original relationship of Life and of the First Living Being. It is also this which explains alternately the extreme humility with which the Son approaches the Father, but also, as an inevitable consequence of their unity, *the belonging to the Son of all that belongs to the Father, in this case, life and the power of giving it* (see below, chapter 10).

We are now in the presence of what we sought: the final legitimation of the words of Christ regarding himself. As long as these words are interpreted as the words of the world in connection with an external referent whose existence they are incapable of establishing, doubt remains. By virtue of being the Word [*Verbe*], however, Christ speaks a completely different word [*parole*], the Word [*Parole*] of Life. He *is* this Word [*Parole*]. Consequently, the Truth of this word ceases to be problematic. The reality that it expresses is in no way foreign to it; it is no more a correlate different from it, whose existence it would be powerless to establish. Just as suffering does not say anything other than suffering, *the reality, of which the Word* [Verbe] *of Life speaks, is Life itself, of which it is the self-revelation, the actual reality:* "In him was Life."

To the extent to which Christ is the Word [*Verbe*] of God, the objections of his enemies regarding what he says concerning himself, namely that he is the Messiah and the Word [*Verbe*], have lost any possible sense. In fact, Christ can only retort to this: "you say, 'He is our God,' though you do not know him. But I know him; if I were to say that I do not know him, I would be a liar like you. But I do know him" (John 8:54-55). Inasmuch as he is actually the Word [*Verbe*], *Christ is nothing other than the knowledge that God has of himself,* according to the rigorous terms to which we have endeavored to hold ourselves, being *the self-revelation of absolute Life.* In this way the legitimation of the words spoken by Christ concerning himself is absolute, like this absolute Life of which he is the self-revelation.

Yet if Christ *is,* as Word [*Verbe*], this self-revelation, which testifies to itself, in such a way that it requires no other witness than itself, does not the question remain open: where does this final legitimacy that Christ is *in himself* reside *for us?* What testimony will we, these living beings who only live a finite life, have at our disposal? His testimony, that of his words? How can we know, we who are not Christ, that Christ is the Word [*Verbe*] and that his words are those of Truth? How, in other words, do we hear the Word [*Parole*] of God, knowing that it is that of God, *knowing that he who speaks it is his Word* [Verbe]? Of the many incontestable difficulties which present themselves here, we understand better that they result from our own condition, that of a finite life which does not carry within itself its own justification.

CHAPTER 9

Christ's Words about the Difficulty for Humans to Hear His Word

That it is difficult for humans to hear the Word [*Parole*] of God is a constant theme in Christ's teaching. It appears as much when Christ speaks to humans in order to tell them about themselves as when he speaks to them about himself. Who would have had to be conscious of this difficulty more than him, who knew humans — "I know . . . you" (John 5:42) — and yet, on the other hand, was one with this Word that he came to make them understand, in order to tear them away from idolatry and to reestablish them in the Covenant? Throughout his public life, Christ comes up against the incomprehension of his listeners. Not only from the especially devious and the hypocrites whose hostility, which very quickly changed into hatred, was to hound him all the way to the end. The humblest, indeed the most naive, obviously had a lot of trouble grasping what he said to them, especially regarding the most crucial revelations. Let us reconsider the conversation with the Samaritan woman to whom Christ declared: "If you knew the gift of God, and who it is that is saying to you, 'Give me a drink,' you would have asked him, and he would have given you living water." We recall the woman's touching response: "Sir, you have no bucket, and the well is deep. Where do you get that living water?" (John 4:10-11). Admittedly, a Pharisee as well-educated as Nicodemus does not appear any more shrewd. When Christ says to him: "Very truly, I tell you, no one can see the kingdom of God without being born from above," Nicodemus replies: "How can anyone be born again after having grown old? Can one enter a second time into the mother's womb and be born?" (John 3:3-4).

It is not the relative intelligence of his interlocutors which leads Christ to resort to the very specific literary form of the parable. It is the nature of the reality about which he wants to instruct them which motivates the reversal of our habitual patterns of thought. The parable stays close to the visible world and employs repeated structures. We have also seen how ordinary language leans heavily on the appearing of this world in which everything this language can name shows itself — if one believe the prejudice, more alive today than ever. Yet, Christ spoke of an invisible life, his own eternal Life, which is also shared with all living beings. The task to which the parables must respond hence opens up to us in all clarity. From an astonishingly brief and often very concise story, happening in the world and told in the language of the world, the parable suggests laws and types of relationships which are no longer those of the world but of life. And it does so in the double sense of this life which we experience in ourselves as our own life and also of that which never ceases to give life to itself and to enable it: eternal Life. The goal of the parable hence is to establish an analogy between two universes, that of the visible and of the invisible, of the finite and of the infinite, in such a way that a series of events occurring in the first prompts us to form a notion of the second, namely the reign of God.

Many of the parables put this structure of analogy into play, which the text expresses directly by saying: "The Kingdom of God is like . . ." "The kingdom of God is as if someone would scatter seed on the ground, and would sleep and rise night and day, and the seed would sprout and grow, he does not know how" (Mark 4:26-27). "The kingdom of heaven is like a mustard seed" (Matt. 13:31-32; cf. Luke 13:18-19; Mark 4:30-32). "The kingdom of heaven is like yeast that a woman took and mixed in with three measures of flour" (Matt. 13:33; Luke 13:20). "The kingdom of heaven is like a treasure hidden in a field, which someone found and hid; then in his joy he goes and sells all that he has and buys that field" (Matt. 13:44).

Other parables, in which the comparison is not explicitly formulated, nevertheless presuppose this analogy. It is always a matter of starting from a state of things or from phenomena which arise from common experience and moving toward what one does not know or has not yet seen, except through a veil, as "an obscure image in a mirror," according to Paul's formulation [see 1 Cor. 13:12]. The purpose of Christ's teaching is unfailing: to elevate the human spirit by detaching it from worldly affairs, whose trademark is transience and vanity, in order to open it to what alone matters.

Yet one parable stands out from the others. It no longer has as its goal the gradual revelation of the reign of God or the manner of reaching it. A preliminary possibility, which defines the aim of our search exactly, is tackled here: namely that of hearing the Word of God, that is to say, of understanding all of the parables through which Christ endeavors to help us form a notion of the secrets of the Kingdom. We find ourselves in the presence of a reflection by Christ on the parables themselves, on their effectiveness, that is to say, when all is said and done, on our ability to grasp their meaning. It is not at all a coincidence that he chooses to uncover in this parable the possibility of hearing the Word of God but also the obstacles which interfere with its hearing.

This is the well-known parable of the sower, a very simple and yet crucial parable, if it is true that on its comprehension depends that of all the others, as Mark's version affirms explicitly: "He said to them also, 'Do you not understand this parable? Then how will you understand all the parables?'" (Mark 4:13). This is the reason Christ is concerned with giving an explanation for it, reported in all three Synoptic Gospels — the importance of which is not disguised by its apparent clarity.

What the sower sows, is actually the Word of God. "The sower sows the word" (Mark 4:14). Luke also says: "The seed is the word of God" (Luke 8:11). Likewise, "When anyone hears the word of the kingdom" (Matt. 13:19). Within the parable, the ground on which the seed falls is presented successively as the edge of the path (where, trampled underfoot, it does not take root and the birds eat it), the rocks (where, devoid of moisture, it withers up and dies), thorns (where it is smothered by their growth), and finally the good earth, where it comes up and bears fruit. *The seed is the Word of God; the place where it is received is our "heart."* The varied nature of the ground hence represents the manifold ways in which the heart behaves in regard to this Word that is constitutive of its being. To the extent that the word shapes the human heart, it is prepared to receive it. The good earth refers to the heart in the purity of its original condition, that of the Son generated in the self-revelation of life. The other situations evoked describe the different forms of evil which distort the original condition of the heart, in such a way that the reception of the Word [*Parole*] cannot be accomplished — much less its performance — and the word is rejected.

In a pithy summary, Christ himself defines the different forms of evil. The first, truly appalling, concerns those who hear the Word, but at the very moment they hear it, the evil arises which obliterates their attention. Everything occurs as if the word had never been spoken, as if it had never been heard — as if the Word [Verbe] came even to his own, but had not been received. Here evil is not some anonymous and impersonal principle, it is someone, it is animated by a will of its own, it pursues a circumscribed end: the deprivation of salvation. Buried in our own heart, free like us, it maybe really is us.

The second form of evil concerns those who, having heard the Word and having received it with joy, have nevertheless not held onto it. Not carrying the strength of the Word in themselves, they are incapable of facing up to adversity and when it occurs unexpectedly, they are immediately "scandalized" (Matt. 13:21 [Gk. *skandalizetai*]). Being scandalized means to revolt when discovering that there is adversity and that this adversity is inflicted on them. For [by their logic] it is obvious that this trial is an evil and that this evil cannot come from the one it scandalizes. From where does it come? From others? But others find themselves in the same situation; they are equally scandalized. Maybe the trial and the evil come from God? The scandal here reaches its limit point. How could God want or at least permit such a thing? How can one believe in God after Auschwitz? Thus, God does not exist. So humans are left with the trial, with the evil, with Auschwitz, on their hands. There is no longer a third to accuse! No longer anything or anyone before whom or by whom to be scandalized — except humanity. And it is really so. According to the affirmation of a humble priest of the diocese of Nantes, God is not concerned with human affairs; God speaks to the heart. In Christ's dazzling parable, to be scandalized means: to accuse, to unleash the tumult of hatred in one's heart, to cast anathema against the other and precisely against God, who does not exist, and because of all this no longer to hear his Word!

We are then referred to the third form of evil, the most immediate and the most widespread, also the one which allows us to see its deep-rootedness in the heart the most clearly.[1] If the very givenness of our own life lies in the self-givenness of absolute Life, its self-revelation in our Self which is also our heart, then this givenness is really that of a life which is particular to us, is our own, that of a singular self that is mine — or yours — which belongs to me forever, to whom this life forever belongs: "If you knew the gift of God."

This gift is so extraordinary and marvelous that we must recognize it in its simplest and most concrete forms. Let us consider as an example the powers of our flesh, such as we live them in our daily existence. For one, the subjective power of prehension — that of taking hold of an object, of picking it up, of throwing it — or even the power of movement, of getting up, of walking, and so forth. The exercise of each of these powers appears to me under the form of an objective performance — for example the moving of my hand toward an object that it wants to grab hold of — but this is only its appearance in the "outside" of the world. In itself, the bringing into play of any bodily power is a subjective activity felt inwardly and lived in a feeling of effort. It is accomplished in us in our flesh and belongs to it. Being in a position to exercise a power, being in possession of the capacity of power, "being able to have power [*pouvoir pouvoir*]" as Kierkegaard says, is only possible for someone who, established at the interior of this power and being one with it, finds him- or herself thus capable of causing it to take action each time and as often as he or she wants to — freely. This freedom is not an abstract idea, a gratuitous affirmation; it is this concrete power, actually experienced and lived by putting into play all of the powers that are thus available to us. Our freedom is one with that fundamental 'I can' which inhabits each of the powers of our flesh but also of our mind (such as forming an image, a concept, interrupting an association of ideas, etc.). These various powers only differ among themselves by their specific content, but the capacity of power inherent in each of them permitting its move to action is common to them.

---

1. [Henry departs from his elucidation of the parable of the sower here, having mentioned the third form of evil — associated in the text of Matthew 13 as "thorns" representing "the cares of this world, and the lure of riches." The text serves as a platform for his broader analysis of the way in which sin and evil (including notably the failure to acknowledge the source of one's own life) prevent the hearing of the Word of God. He will return to the parable of the sower in chapter 10.]

Yet how are these various powers and especially that of exercising them given to me, in such a way that they are mine, those of my own life? That is not an artificial question if one reflects on this indisputable situation: I who have each of these powers at my disposal — opening my eyes, holding out my hand, moving myself — I have not given them to myself, any more than I have given my own self or my own life to myself. Thus I am constrained to recognize my total powerlessness with regard to each of these powers as much as with regard to the fundamental power which allows me to deploy them, if it is true that they are given to me independently of my power and of my willing. How are they given to me? In the same manner as my own life and my own self: in the self-givenness of absolute Life.

Christ categorically affirms this radical powerlessness of humans in respect to their own power even though they exercise and experience it. Formulated in a tragic circumstance, it assumes a solemn character which underlines its universal scope. We know how, at the time of the final trial, Pilate brandishes his threat before Christ who stays obstinately silent, so as to get Christ to speak and without doubt to save himself: "Do you not know that I have power to release you and power to crucify you?" The answer is stinging: "You would have no power over me unless it had been given you from above" (John 19:10-11). Conceding nothing, Christ refers not only to the impotence of the power of the emperor, but of any power, even that governing the simplest of gestures: "Apart from me you can do nothing" (John 15:5). Paul will develop this fundamental theme of Christianity on several occasions: "For it is God who is at work in you, enabling you both to will and to work for his good pleasure" (Phil. 2:13).

This powerlessness of humans, even within the actual exercise of their 'I can,' signifies their condition of sonship — the fact that each of their powers, that their self, that their lives are only given to themselves in the self-givenness of absolute Life. Yet this gift is not the simulacrum of a gift; it is a genuine gift, that of an actual life, of a real self, of real powers. Lived in the indubitable experience that they have of themselves in their free exercise, they are experienced as actually free, and they are free indeed. Consequently, the I which constantly lives the extraordinary capacity of putting each of these powers into play whenever it wants, easily imagines itself to be their source. It thinks that it is itself who provides them, that it draws them in some manner from itself each time it exercises them. Source and grounding of all the powers which make up its being, *it deems itself finally to be the source and the foundation of its very being.* Thus the greatest illusion of all: this I, insuperably passive toward itself, always already given to itself in life, placed in it independently of its own willing, has become in its own eyes an all-powerful Subject, master of itself, as it were an absolute principle of its condition of living, of its self, of all its capacities and its talents. "My life belongs to me," or, as one says today, "My body is mine. And consequently I do with it as I want." Paul's warning arises in vain: "What do you have that you did not receive? And if you received it, why do you boast as if it were not a gift?" (1 Cor. 4:7). To attribute to oneself not only the disposal of powers one finds in oneself but the power of giving all these powers to oneself, and, finally, that of giving oneself, in one's own life, this self that one is — that is the truly insane belief that Paul also denounces: "For if those who are nothing think they are something, they deceive themselves" (Gal. 6:3).

The illusion which makes the ego its own foundation does not merely distort the manner in which humans represent themselves to themselves, and therefore their relationship to the world and to things. It completely subverts the place where we are given to ourselves in absolute Life, namely our "heart." If we conceal this internal relationship to the divine Life in which the heart is engendered and in which it remains as long as it lives, then it becomes blind in regard to itself. Deaf to the Word of Life which continually speaks of itself at the same time as it continually speaks to the heart of its own life, its perfect life. Insensitive to the urges of love that Life communicates to it. Hardened and rejected in itself, enclosed in this monadic ego which takes itself henceforth as the only reality, placing itself at the center of all that happens to it — so that no possible experience is any longer its own, but that of a finite ego. This heart blind to Truth, deaf to the Word of Life, full of hardness, exclusively preoccupied with itself, taking itself as the point of departure and the end of its experiences and of its actions: that is the source of evil.

If one rereads in Mark and in Matthew the list of the evils that spring from the heart, it is striking to observe that they are all in keeping with what we have called "the human system" which is in truth a system of egotism. Each of them, in fact — murder, adultery, theft, false testimony, slander, and so forth — enter the round of reciprocity that we have seen does not possess any value in itself, since it is as much a reciprocity of hatred, resentment, or envy as it is of kindness or love. Yet why are all the modalities of existence cited in these passages a matter of evil? This is due to what the analysis of the subversion of the human heart has taught us. Discounting the interior connection to the life in which it is engendered, the I takes itself as this ego-subject which subsists in itself and does not owe anything to anyone. Placing itself at the center of the field of its experiences — those which it has of itself, of its body, of others — it may well hurl itself toward everything that preoccupies it in the world, making of them as many idols. Referring all reality back to itself, and seeking in all things only its own pleasure, it is really itself that it idolizes. Everywhere reciprocity is an illusion — as, for example, in eroticism, which becomes merely an auto-eroticism for two. And even when it lowers and demeans itself in masochism, it is still itself, it is still its questionable pleasure that alone matters to it. As long as everyone acts in such a way, egoism, as we have pointed out, is not a simple character trait, but belongs to the system of evil of which it embodies one of the major forms.

Yet this evil will increase immeasurably. And here is how. The illusion that the I creates about itself, taking itself as the source of the power that it exercises, does not change anything in the fact that this power, for the same reason as this self and its own life, are only given to it in the self-givenness of absolute Life. This self-givenness is a self-revelation that is itself absolute. It is invisible light and absolute Truth which shines its light into every recess of the heart. Its distinctive trait is violence — violence against which there is no protection.

Christ has taught us about this Truth of life, applying to himself a certain crucial characteristic. It is because Life is the violence of a self-revelation — without caution or retreat, delay or oration — that, revealing itself in the lightning-flash of the eternal Coming [*Parousia*], it immediately bears witness to itself. Yet the Truth of absolute Life is not only the condition for absolute witness — needing no other testimony — but also for Judgment. This is the Judgment of God from which no one escapes, whose truth is in the Truth of absolute Life; in its insuperable self-revelation each I is revealed in its heart. Thus, *the Judgment is not different from the coming of each Self in itself, and accompanies it as long as it lives.* And as the self-revelation of the Life in each living Self dwells in each of the modalities of its life, its joys, its injuries, the actions which result from them, so are each of these actions, in the very moment in which they are accomplished, known to God, as well as their motives, whether respectable or not. That is why this Judgment from which no one escapes is relentless. And the superiority of Cain over people of our time is that he knew what the grace of an unthinkable pardon might be. He knew it when he turned his face away from God's anger. For he too was a son, not of Adam and of Eve, but of Light.

Among the most terrifying of Christ's words are those which denounce the hatred of truth. We have come to understand at whom this hatred is directed. If each modality of our life, each movement of our heart is revealed to it in the self-revelation of absolute Life, then any evil, jealous, hostile, or criminal thought and any action which results from it, finds itself exposed. It is John again who reports these irrevocable words in the conversation with Nicodemus: "For all who do evil hate the light and do not come to the light, so that their deeds may not be exposed" (John 3:20). Yet this Light which is the Truth of absolute Life, which bears testimony and renders Judgment, what is it other than the self-revelation of this Life in its Word [*Verbe*]? The Word [*Verbe*] of God, of which the Prologue says: The Word [*Verbe*] was "the true light which enlightens everyone coming into the world. He was in the world, and the world came into being through him; yet the world did not know him. He came to what was his own, and his own people did not accept him" (John 1:9-11). It is because the Word [*Verbe*] is the unmitigated revelation that illuminates the secret of the heart that humans devoted to evil hate the Word [*Verbe*]. This Word [*Verbe*] has come into the world to bring the True Light and to save the world. Thus, salvation has become condemnation for those who have refused this Light. This is what the context of the conversation says: "And this is the judgment, that the light has come into the world, and people loved darkness rather than light because their deeds were evil. For all who do evil hate the light" (John 3:19-20).

The Gospel of John goes back to this hatred of the Word [*Verbe*] which came into the world in order to save it, as to a haunting theme. As we know, Christ is condemned to death for the first time after the resurrection of Lazarus. He goes into hiding, withdraws to Galilee, avoids

Judea and the Jewish authorities who are seeking to seize and kill him. His relatives, who do not believe in him, press him to make himself known in his works and to manifest himself to all [John 7:3-5]. That means to go to Jerusalem where death awaits him. This is when Christ himself defines his relationship to the world in all clarity: "My time has not yet come, but your time is always here. The world cannot hate you, but it hates me because I testify against it that its works are evil" (John 7:6-7). John goes on to say that this hatred of the True Light incarnate in Christ becomes extended to all those who, having received it, become sons of Light, bearing their own witness in turn: "If the world hates you, be aware that it hated me before it hated you. If you belonged to the world, the world would love you as its own. Because you do not belong to the world, but I have chosen you out of the world — therefore the world hates you." This hatred of Christ, which all those who have received him will in turn suffer, is in reality a hatred of the True Light of which Christ is the Word [Parole]. The text goes on to affirm this: "Whoever hates me hates my Father also. If I had not done among them the works that no one else did, they would not have sin. But now they have seen and hated both me and my Father." Thus the word written in their law is accomplished: "They hated me without a cause" (John 15:18-19, 23-25).

So it is that evil becomes sin when it enters into the light of Truth. In sin, in some way, evil intensifies. Far from recognizing itself as evil in the glory of this devastating Light, evil blames that very Light. This is what happens in the scandal.[2] With only the relentless Light to expose it, the scandal, by reversing the indictment, pushes evil to its limit, to the supreme sin, which is no longer simple evil, but the denunciation of Light, the negation of God.

Meanwhile, the Light continues to burn in the heart of Cain with an ember that never goes out. In its incandescent radiance, it not only consumes a self; it glows in the splendor of the eternal Coming [Parousia]. The Word [Verbe] has become incarnate to save what was lost. How then is it still possible for humans to hear his Word [Parole], despite, beyond, and through evil?

---

2. [Cf. Matt. 13:21, and the argument earlier in the chapter about those who are "scandalized" when evil presents itself and, as a result, accuse God.]

CHAPTER 10

Christ's Words about the Possibility
for Humans to Hear His Word

When we confronted in Christ's most astounding words, those making him equal to his Father, the problem of their legitimacy (a problem posed continually by his hecklers), I chose to interrupt the analysis of their content. Faced with a difficulty that would seem insurmountable to us, would it not be a good idea to question, no longer the supposedly blasphemous content, but rather the nature of the Word [*Parole*] uttering it? Would it not present itself as a radically different word, whose origin is elsewhere: the Word [*Parole*] of God? Is it not precisely this Word [*Parole*] which can justify the statements in which Christ calls himself the Word [*Verbe*] of God, his Word [*Parole*]?

Reflecting on the nature of the word [*parole*] considered in itself, we have seen how and why it has been interpreted traditionally as "word of the world." In the eyes of the majority of people, this word of the world is the one they speak since they were first taught to speak. This is the word they think, which permits them to communicate with each other. It is this identification of the human word with the word of the world that I have denounced.[1] If humans are living beings generated in life, if they are its sons, do they not besides the capacity to speak the things of the

---

1. [This distinction between the "human word" and the "word of the world" is crucial to an understanding of the very dense argument that follows. Whereas the "word of the world," in its materiality, opposes the "word of life," the "human word" is informed by it, shaped by it, taking its meaning from it, even when this is neither understood nor acknowledged. "The human word can in no way be reduced to a word of the world; it is first that of life."]

world, made possible because of their openness to that world, necessarily carry within themselves a more ancient word, that of the life in which they are revealed to themselves and which continues to make of them living beings? How can we dispute this presence of the word of life in us? Do humans not speak constantly of themselves? For example, in a phrase like the following: "After what has happened, I feel increasingly discouraged." Considered objectively, such a statement assuredly belongs to the language of the world. It is composed of words [*mots*], carriers of meaning, which relate to external referents: on the one hand, the events to which he has alluded; on the other hand, this individual, who stands in the room and has just expressed his discouragement to his wife or a friend.

Yet we have already been constrained to ask this question: from where do these significations come? Would it be possible to form the signification "discouragement" if, somewhere else than in a "world," something like a discouragement was not itself experienced in the immanent and emotive self-revelation of life? Similarly, from where does this "self," this "I" which calls itself discouraged, come — if not, as John's Prologue shows, from the inner movement by which absolute Life engenders itself in generating the First Self in which it experiences itself, without which no life, no living being, no "me" would be conceivable? Thus, while the word of the world prattles on, linking its significations without any end assigned to its discourse, a different word has already spoken in us. This Word of Life which continually speaks to everyone his or her own life, may also be expressed (or not) in the language of conversation which is also that of written texts, of books — of the Scriptures.

Yet, this precedence of the word of life is not only acknowledged when individuals speak of themselves. Usually they are so preoccupied with events of this world that their talk traces along these lines, becoming confused by the many details. Even then, the Word of Life does not cease to speak under this mundane talk and to support it secretly. Consider the following: "The road in front of the house is completely torn up; it will become impassable." This statement speaks not about a "thing," a thing of the world, but about a thing of life, an object for a task, the reply to a need. As the word of the world remains prisoner of the visible universe, rather than succumbing to hebetude before the many goods and benefits which it intentionally dangles before our desires, it is these desires themselves we must return to if we want to understand something about ordinary human activity and what people are saying.

This constant reference of the word of the world to a word which precedes it and of which it is only an expression, although often distorted, suffices to blow up the most ancient prejudice concerning language. *The human word can in no way be reduced to a word of the world; it is first that of life.* It is thus that a first difficulty disappears concerning the possibility for us to comprehend Christ's final words about himself, in which he identifies himself with the Word [*Verbe*]. One can say, in fact, in accordance with Christ's teaching, that human beings are the sons of God, that is, let me repeat it, to say that they draw their condition of living from their birth in life. They are living beings in life, experiencing themselves in multiple impressions, emotions, actions, and thoughts, given to themselves in the self-revelation of absolute Life, that is to say in its Word [*Verbe*]. How could one not henceforth carry this Word of Life in oneself, which is at work in everything one feels, whether one speaks about oneself or about things of the world or whether one is silent?

No longer does a chasm gape between the Word of Christ — especially by which he declares himself to be the Word [*Verbe*] — and the word which speaks in us. Quite to the contrary, they are linked to each other by a decisive affinity, since both are words of Life. Is it not this very affinity which unites living beings to the life which lives in them and continues to give them life — between the son of God and God himself? Such an affinity is not built progressively during the course of our history; it does not result from our efforts, but makes them possible. It is registered in our timeless birth, in this coming of each one of us into ourselves, which is our revelation to ourselves in the self-revelation of life. Whoever is born of life hears the Word [*Parole*] of Life. Paul's initiatory text unveils this native predestination of everyone to hear this Word [*Parole*]: "For those whom he foreknew he also predestined to be conformed to the image of his Son, in order that he might be the firstborn within a large family. And those whom he predestined *he also called*" (Romans 8:29-30; emphasis mine).

That this affinity between the status of son and the hearing of the Word [*Parole*] takes place in the beginning explains how it spans the Old

Testament before being received in its full revelation in the Word of Christ. As an example let us consider the extraordinary dialogue between God and Cain: "Where is your brother Abel?" God knows what Cain has done, how he has killed Abel, where he has hidden his body. It is in fact in the self-revelation of absolute Life that the self-revelation constitutive of Cain's "heart" is accomplished, making him the one who knows what he does, feels, and experiences. In this way, all that Cain knows — all he does, feels, and experiences — God also knows. To say it in the fashion of the mystics: the Eye by which God sees Cain and the one by which Cain sees himself are but one and the same Eye. As Christ's indelible maxim affirms in its simplicity: "God sees in secret." God knows all that Cain knows, precisely because the knowledge that Cain has of himself is none other than the knowledge that God has of Cain. This is the very reason Cain also knows. Struck literally in the heart by God's violent word, Cain attempts to face up to it. His supremely insolent remark proceeds from his confusion: "Am I my brother's keeper?" Yet how can he escape a constitutive truth of his being? Cain hides his face and, in order to separate himself from a truth which is both that of God and at the same time his own, devoid of any tie on earth as in heaven, he drifts into a ceaseless roaming across what has no other name than "the outer darkness."

The identity of the immediate understanding that Cain has of the Word of God showing his crime to him with the understanding he has of himself, unquestionably has a general significance. It demonstrates the possibility, in principle, for humans to understand the Word of God. Yet the term 'understanding' is really inappropriate here. For what is at stake is not knowledge in the usual sense. The comprehension takes place in a sequence of ideas, of significations, which become valid from the moment where one can perceive them in an evidence which arises from seeing, that is to say of the word of the world. Humans have a completely different possibility of hearing the Word of God if it resides in their status as sons of God or, as we still say, in their timeless birth. It means that coming into the condition of experiencing oneself and of being revealed to oneself is accomplished in the self-revelation of absolute Life in its Word [*Verbe*]. In other words, the possibility that humans have to hear the Word [*Parole*] of God is consubstantial with them. And this concerns in the first place the Word [*Parole*] of Christ inasmuch as it is Word [*Verbe*], this Word [*Parole*] of Life in which any living being happens to itself. Henceforth, the legitimacy of the Word [*Parole*] of Christ speaking about himself and affirming that he is the Word [*Verbe*] is not only grounded for him in his own status as the Word [*Verbe*]. It is valid also for all those in whom this Word [*Parole*] speaks — for all the sons.

A difficulty which seemed insurmountable to us is then resolved. That being said, however, one difficulty has given way to another. This place of their timeless birth, where all of the sons are revealed to themselves in the self-revelation of absolute Life in its Word [*Verbe*], is their heart. But this is the heart from which evil comes forth. The various parables which concern this evil, especially the parable of the sower, have described its different modes. A strange reversal happens when in its limited form evil is categorically referred to as "sin." The Truth of the word which illuminates the heart and constructs its inner relationship with God all of a sudden runs counter to this relationship. This is why the incredible antithesis Christ throws in the face of his hecklers has an effect: *"But because I tell the truth, you do not believe me"* (John 8:45; emphasis mine).

I have already analyzed the reading Christ himself gives of this difficult text. It unmasks the fact that evil rejects Truth. Let me add this remark: Although evil has come to hate truth, it has not severed all link with it. To the contrary, it is this link that motivates its hatred. In this way the relationship of the heart to Truth stills defines the abyss. Let us now suppose that this relationship would be restored to its original purity, the heart to its timeless birth in the Word of Life. In any case, whether evil breathes hatred in its heart or whether it recovers its native purity, the relationship of the living being to life and of the heart to the Word which engenders it, depends on the nature of this Word in which all has been made. We must deepen this connection.

Let me return one more time to the opposition of the Word of Life to that of the world. The latter speaks of what shows itself in the exteriority of the world; it refers to an external content whose existence it is incapable of positing. The Word of Life, in contrast, owes nothing to the world. The power of revelation on which it relies is that of life — the Word of Life being but its self-revelation, its Word [*Verbe*]. It follows that the

Word [*Parole*] of Life speaks, not of things of the world, but of Life itself. Or, to put it more precisely, it speaks life. What it says, it never puts outside of itself; it guards it as a good never to be discarded, since it is its own life.

This singular situation concerns our own finite life as much as the absolute Life of God. In fact, just as absolute Life experiences itself in the First Self living in this way, that Life remains in him as he remains in it, so each living being, only given to itself in this self-revelation of Life in its Word [*Verbe*], remains in it as it remains in him. Because the immanence of Life in each living being cannot be severed as long as it lives, all living beings find themselves constituted in themselves as the ones who, at the moment itself of their timeless birth, but also as long as they will actually live, hearing in themselves the Word of Life which, never ceasing to give them to themselves, does not cease to speak their life to them.

One will object: what human being hears such a word in him- or herself? Would it be like Joan of Arc of whom one said that "she heard voices"? This ironic question, like other more vehement ones, such as that of the Pharisees to Christ: "Where is your Father?" (John 8:19), or even more tragic contemporary statements, pretending to be simple observations, like Kafka's "Heaven is silent, it is only the echo of silence," have forgotten only one thing: *the nature of the Word* which they accuse of silence and which yet speaks but in a completely different manner from what they think, so that they do not actually hear anything.

Hearing, listening: we understand these terms first by giving them a limited or naive meaning. Hearing, listening means for us to hear with our ears, with the sense of hearing. The sense of hearing, however, can only hear what resonates outside of us, in the world: sounds, whether noises of this world or the words [*mots*] humans exchange and which are also part of the complex of sounds perceived in the world. Likewise with sight, one sees only what becomes visible before us, in the world. With the sense of touch, one only touches what is given to sense, to touch, outside of us, in the world. Our senses are all powers that thrust us into the world, opening us to it and to all that shows itself in it, outside of ourselves. Hearing, listening, thus understood, are the modes of the word of the world — which speaks to us of what shows itself to us outside, in the world. In this way, before we are able to hear what it says to us, the word of the world speaks, allowing it to be heard in the world. Speaking means in this case to utter sounds thanks to the organ of speech. It is only when such sounds have been produced by us or by others that we can hear them, and eventually listen to them. In the same way as hearing or listening, speaking is here a mode of the word of the world. Speaking in this sense means taking the word, raising the voice, making it resonate *in the world* in such a way that, sounding and resounding in it, it is able to be heard. In all cases, the appearing which is the condition of both the spoken and the heard word, is nothing other than this appearing of the world.

The Word of Life is totally different. In its self-revelation, it speaks of itself and this, we have seen, in each of its modes. Suffering says its suffering; anguish, its anguish. It speaks about itself, never about anything else, never about the world. But first *it does not speak in the world*. It is also impossible to hear it there. The word of life is inaudible. No one has ever heard it in the way in which one hears a noise of the world, a sound which resonates in it. No one has ever heard it with his or her ears, by using the sense of hearing. Who ever heard his suffering or her joy by using the sense of hearing? *One does not gain access to life, to one's own life, to that of others, or to that of God, by means of the senses.* Those who enter convents in order to hear the word of God better, do not hope to hear it the way they would hear the noise of the fountain in the courtyard of the cloister, or the silence of the courtyard when the fountain has been turned off. The silence of the cloister is only the occasion, by silencing the noises of the world, for hearing a different silence — which is not caused by the reduction of the number of decibels, or by their absence. It is not a silence where there is no noise; it is *a silence where there cannot be any,* because, where it is established, no sense is at work, no ear. And it is thus that no sound is possible anymore. Even so, this silence is not that of muteness. Fullness of life speaks in it, seamless and faultless.

Where does life speak? In the heart. How? In its emotive immediate self-revelation. In the heart is held every constituent of this structure of self-revelation that defines human reality: impressions, desires, emotions, wants, feelings, actions, thoughts. The "heart" is the only adequate definition of the human. Everything foreign to this phenomenal structure of self-revelation — the material, in its multiple forms and its various structures — does not belong to the human order.

Yet Christ's teaching repeats tirelessly that everything that pulsates within the human heart — these emotions, these desires, these actions — do not for all that constitute an autonomous whole. The tonalities in which our life expresses itself are incapable of giving themselves life. The Self which inhabits them is also devoid of the power of bringing itself into this self that it is. This inherent powerlessness can be recognized in each of its powers, none of which has given itself the power of exercising it. "You would have no power over me, if it had not been given to you from above." The powers of our life and our Self are finite. We know this, but we also experience what it means: they are only given to themselves in the self-givenness of absolute Life, which is his Word.

To give our life to itself, and our Self to itself — and that in the self-revelation of pathos — means that absolute Life must engender them. In this way divine Life repeats for each living being the work that it has accomplished for itself, generating the First Self in whom, experiencing itself, it has revealed itself in this self-revelation which is his Word. A new characteristic of the word then opens up to us: *its omnipotence.* This decisive trait of the Word of the Word [*Parole du Verbe*] illuminates the entire life of Christ. It alone explains *why there is no difference between the word of Christ and his action.* Because of this omnipotence, each of Christ's words is identically an action, while each of his actions, even if not accompanied by any commentary, acts as a revelation.

Thus, word and action go together in the episode of the leper who comes to prostrate himself before Jesus. "Then he stretched out his hand, touched him, and said, 'I do choose. Be made clean!'" (Luke 5:13; cf. Mark 1:40-41; Matt. 8:2-5). The word alone intervenes when the royal official at Capernaum begs Christ to come heal his dying son. Jesus answers him: "'Go; your son will live.' *The man believed the word that Jesus spoke to him*" (John 4:46-53; emphasis mine). The power of the word alone appears even more evident in the story of the healing of the centurion's servant: "Lord, I am not worthy to have you come under my roof, but *only speak the word*" (Luke 7:6-7; cf. Matt. 8:8; emphasis mine). On other occasions, such as the wedding at Cana, the role of the word is limited to brief practical instructions. "Fill the jars with water. . . . Take it to the chief steward" (John 2:1-8). Finally, at times, as in the washing of the feet, the action in its extreme simplicity seems to be sufficient unto itself. Even so, it is followed by a prophetic and mysterious speech at the end of which the Word suddenly refers back to itself, to the omnipotence of him who speaks: "I tell you this now, before it occurs, so that when it does occur, you may believe that *I am* he" (John 13:19).

It is on account of this omnipotence that belongs to him — inasmuch as it is that of the Word [*Verbe*] — that the Word [*Parole*] of Christ is so radically opposed to that of the world. The property of the word of the world, as we have said, is its incapacity to bring into existence the external content to which it refers; although open to the world, it speaks of things of the world without being able to create them. Inasmuch as it is that of the Word [*Verbe*], however, the word of Christ is not distinguished only from that of the world. We have seen in fact how, far from being reduced to this word of the world, the human word is first a word of life. In its simplest forms, our language handles multiple meanings which come forth from life, as when we say: "I am hungry," "I am bored," "I am scared," and so forth. But our life is finite, devoid of power to give life to itself. *For this reason, its word is also finite, incapable of bestowing reality on that about which it speaks.* It is not the person who says: "I am, I exist, I see," who has brought him- or herself into the marvelous condition of being alive. Quite the contrary: he or she must already be in life in order to be in a position to formulate for him- or herself any proposition of the sort we have cited. One must also recognize that the word of life, to the extent that it concerns a life like ours, remains marked by the same powerlessness with respect to itself as the word of the world does with respect to things.

In contrast, there is an aura of limitless power that springs forth each time the word of Christ is spoken, provoking amazement everywhere around it. This power takes on a cosmic character when Christ commands the storm to be stilled. Just as the extraordinary content of the Beatitudes leads those who hear them to wonder about the person whose omniscience surpasses any human knowing, so the no less extraordinary power linked to his word in turn produces the question about him who holds such authority. "And they said to one another: 'Who then is this, that even the wind and the sea obey him?'" (Mark 4:41; cf. Matt. 13:27). It is this same mysterious power over the hidden essence of things which shows through in the episode where we see Peter sinking in the waves, calling for the Lord's help (Matt. 14:25-33), or in the great "signs" of changing the water into wine at Cana or the multiplication of bread.

Most often, however, the power of Christ is exercised on the heart, aiming to produce in it a radical transformation, a "purification." At stake is the elimination of evil and of the restoration, in the very place where it is fulfilled, of the original relationship of the living being with God. It is thus that the alteration made to the order of things — the sudden termination in an illness, of a disability, indeed of death — is in fact only the "sign" of Christ's omnipotence. Finally, it refers to the inevitable mediation of the Word [*Verbe*] in any generation of a living being into life. Life only becomes itself in the Self of the First Living Being whom it generates in itself as its Word [*Verbe*]. Each living being in turn only experiences itself in the Self of this Word [*Verbe*]. This is how the Prologue puts it: "All things came into being through him, and without him not one thing came into being" (John 1:3).

This subordination of the transformation of things to the purification of the heart, and ultimately to the generation of the living being in the omnipotence of the Word [*Verbe*] of God, emerges from one of the crucial Gospel episodes, that of the paralytic to whom Christ has just said: "Your sins are forgiven you." We know the reply (preserved across the centuries) Christ gives to the Pharisees who accuse him of blasphemy, "Who can forgive sins but God alone?" He asks: "Which is easier, to say: 'Your sins are forgiven you' or to say: 'Stand up and walk'?" The healing of the paralytic is thus only the sign of a more originary work, that of forgiveness: "So that you may know that the Son of Man has power on earth to forgive sins." And this is what Christ then says to the paralytic: "I say to you, stand up" (Luke 5:20-24; cf. Mark 2:5-11; Matt. 11:3-6). Forgiving sins is done in such a way that what has been is no longer, and what is not, or never has been, is made to exist, restored to its initial splendor. The power to forgive sins, as the Pharisees argue, is actually God's prerogative. And Christ has just been revealed to hold such power, giving life, restoring it where it has been disfigured or lost.

Christ claims this power here by identifying himself indisputably with the all-powerful Word of God. It is here also that, accomplishing this gift of life, his Word [*Parole*] allows the inconceivable power to become visible which no human has ever had at his or her disposal. His statements are final. "Anyone who hears my word. . . has eternal life" (John 5:24). "The hour is coming, and is now here, when the dead will hear the voice of the Son of Man, and those who hear will live" (5:25). "Whoever keeps my word will never see death" (8:51). To the sheep of the parable of the shepherd: "I give them eternal life" (10:28). Because the Word of Life possesses the unthinkable power of giving life, it is an action, the action of giving this life: of engendering it in the timeless birth of any living being, and of reviving it when it is no longer. It is in this way that Christ, raising great fear, brings back to life the son of a widow of Nain, and later the daughter of Jairus, the head of the synagogue. Finally there is the resurrection of Lazarus and the timeless word spoken to Martha: "I am the resurrection and the life. Those who believe in me, even though they die, will live, and everyone who lives and believes in me will never die" (John 11:25-26). Thus throughout Jesus' historical existence the promise made to the Samaritan woman is repeated — this promise that the Word of Life fulfills since the beginning of time and which is the gift of a life free from any finitude: "Those who drink of the water that I will give them will never be thirsty. The water that I will give will become in them a spring of water gushing up to eternal life" (John 4:14).

The Word [*Verbe*] being the Word [*Parole*] of life, it is never separated from it. One also sees the unity of the Word [*Verbe*] and of God, which forms one of the essential themes of Christ's word about himself, reaffirmed by him each time that his amazing power of giving life is exercised. For this power is no other than that of absolute Life to come into life, to engender itself in engendering the Son. Thus the power that the Son displays is the very power that the Father exhibits in him, in such a way that they are both at work in the eternal generation of life. This is the point of the severe reply Christ gives to the ridiculous legalism of the Pharisees who reproach him for having healed a paralytic on the sabbath day — after they have reproached the man healed on this very day for carrying his mat! "Jesus said to them: 'My Father is still working, and I also am working'" (John 5:17). In this way John transmits one of Christ's major revelations to us: his identity with the Father and his own divinity is accomplished in his total subordination to the Father, in his most extreme humility. "Very truly, I tell you, the Son can do nothing on his own, but only what he sees the Father doing; for whatever the Father does, the

Son does likewise. . . . Just as the Father raises the dead and gives them life, so also the Son gives life to whomever he wishes" (John 5:19-21). One must then reinstate verse 24 in its entirety: "Anyone who hears my word and believes him who sent me has eternal life," and add verse 25 — "the dead will hear the voice of the Son of God, and those who hear will live" — and verse 26: "For just as the Father has life in himself, so he has granted the Son also to have life in himself." It is after having recalled his immanence in the all-powerful Life of the Father in several other passages — "I can do nothing on my own" (verse 30) — that Christ, whose word is continually discovered with increasing evidence to be that of the Word [*Verbe*], claims the totality of the Father's powers: "All mine are yours and yours are mine" (John 17:10). Then follow the great lyrical statements, already cited, which celebrate the immanence of the all-powerful Life in the Word [*Verbe*] in which it experiences itself and loves itself eternally, as Christ experiences and loves his Father eternally, in the reciprocal interiority of Love which constitutes the origin and the principle of all life.

Yet the Gospel is not a metaphysical treatise on the internal dynamism of the divine Life. It is turned toward humans. The Incarnation of the Word [*Verbe*] took place for them; the Word [*Parole*] of God is intended for them. If among the words addressed to humans some of them are heard speaking not about themselves but about Christ, that is because these are necessary to justify what he tells them, which is in fact very strange. Yet the essential reason concerns their salvation, because it is itself their salvation — a salvation which consists in sharing unending joy with all living beings, arising from the reciprocal interiority of Life and the First Living One.

In one of his final prayers to the Father, Christ requested this extension of the interior relation of love between the Father and the Son to all living beings: that their communion of love would recapture all those who, born of Life, are called to revive in themselves the eternal process of generation of the Living Beings in Life. Their status as sons will be thus fulfilled, as sensed in the dazzling vision of Meister Eckhart thirteen centuries later: "God engenders himself as myself," "God engenders me as himself" (Sermon #6).

Let us recall some fragments of this final prayer: "Holy Father, protect them in your name that you have given me, so that they may be one, as we are one. . . . I ask not only on behalf of these, but also on behalf of those who will believe in me through their word, that they may all be one. As you, Father, are in me and I am in you, may they also be in us. . . . The glory that you have given me I have given them, so that they may be one, as we are one, I in them and you in me, that they may become completely one" (John 17:11, 20-23).

At the approach of death, which helps to give it its poignant tone, the word of Christ has thus taken the form of a prayer. Would his omnipotence all of a sudden be caught out? Must not any word, even that of God, be heard? The possibility for humans to hear the Word of God resides in their status as sons, open to this word in its timeless birth. That in them which refuses to hear is, without doubt, evil — but also the freedom given to them at the same time as their life. We have seen that Christ has no illusions regarding the hearing reserved for his word: "Many are called, but few are chosen" (Matt. 22:14). Before concluding, we must ask one more time about this hearing of the Word by humans.

Listening to the Word:
What Christ Said in the Synagogue of Capernaum

Christ has legitimized the extraordinary statements that he formulated regarding himself — essentially claims of his divine status. This is manifested in multiple ways and notably in the nature of his word which is that of God. In Johannine language, Christ is the Word [*Verbe*]. Thus his unity with God is affirmed. Speaking not as a human, not searching for his own glory, but *speaking the Word* [Parole] *of God, being his Word* [Verbe], he is discovered to co-belong to the eternal process by which absolute Life occurs by revealing himself in his Word [*Parole*]. In the words he has spoken about himself, after all, it is this Word that speaks to say what it is.

The legitimacy of Christ's affirmation of his divine status hence does not rest in any way on a human word, which would always be suspect. It is not because Christ says, with terms that we employ daily in our language, "I am in the Father and the Father is in me," that this proposition is true in the domain of absolute reality which is that of God. Quite the contrary: it is because it is thus in the absolute reality of the divine essence, eternally thus. It is because, in Life's generation within it of the First Living One, experiencing itself in him, Life reveals itself to itself in the self-revelation which is his Word [*Verbe*], his Word [*Parole*]. It is for this reason alone that this Word, Arch-revelation of divine Life, is in itself Truth, this original and absolute Truth on which everything else depends.

The Word of Christ is, then, not only a Word of Life in its structural contrast to any word of the world — a word foreign to the world, without external referent, speaking about itself, keeping what it says within itself,

114

speaking life in the way in which suffering speaks suffering and joy speaks joy. The Word [*Parole*] of Christ, inasmuch as it is that of the Word [*Verbe*], is the Word [*Parole*] of Life: in it this Arch-revelation is accomplished by which, embracing itself, Life engenders itself, makes itself Life. Word [*Parole*] of Life, self-revelation of Life, Word [*Verbe*] of Life, Logos of Life — as says John, summarizing Christ's many affirmations reported after the Prologue.

We thus find ourselves in the presence of our final question. If what Christ says about himself is not a *word about life* which would still have to prove what it says, but it is Life itself — which reveals itself and speaks in his Word [*Verbe*] in such a way that, Word [*Parole*] and revelation of this absolute Life, it is the absolute Truth which bears witness to itself — what does it matter for us, this word which is that of God? What is our relationship to it? Where does it speak? In what fashion? How can we hear it? Are not all these words of Christ, on which we have reflected, transmitted to us via the intermediary of a written text, under the form of a series of propositions? And even if they were spoken by Christ before those who had the privilege of hearing him, without always being aware of it, were they not formulated in human language, whether in Aramaic or Hebrew? Do not all the doubts, then, return? Does not human language, the language of the Scriptures, refer to an external referent whose existence it is incapable of positing? In accordance with ordinary experience, only plausible suggestions can lay claim to our agreement in such a language. Yet when Christ makes his stunning declarations — "Very truly, I tell you, whoever keeps my word will never see death" — do the "Jews" not have every reason to regard him as someone "possessed" [by demons]? And when, exceeding all measure, detaching himself from the human condition, he places himself outside of time, before history — "Before Abraham was, I am" — what else could they, zealous observers of their Law, really do other than go looking for stones? (John 8:51-52; 8:58).

"Everyone who belongs to the truth listens to my voice" (John 18:37, emphasis mine). To Pilate who, in order to test the accusation of the religious leaders, asks him whether he is a king, Christ unexpectedly modifies the meaning of this word, explaining *in what his royalty consists:* to render testimony to the Truth, to cause the Word of God to reign. It is in these precise circumstances that the condition that should permit hu-

mans to listen to the word is posited in an abrupt fashion. And this condition consists in *a decisive affinity between human belonging to the Truth and the nature of the Word which it is a matter of hearing:* the voice of Christ. To understand what is decisive about this affinity would be difficult if we could not take it from Christ's words themselves. Have we not noticed the confluence, all along these reflections, which is established between the teaching he addresses to humans in order to tell them what they are and the one that progressively unveils his divine nature to them? How, then, does "belonging to the truth" permit us to hear the word of Christ, to *receive it as the Word* [Parole] *of the Word* [Verbe], *that is to say of God himself?*

For the human being, belonging to the truth means to be born of Life, of the only Life that exists: the all-powerful Life which engenders itself. It is the Son of this unique Life who can alone give life: "You have only one Father." Because life is self-revelation, it is Truth, the original and absolute Truth, in relation to which any other truth is merely secondary. Because they are sons of this Life which is Truth, humans belong to the Truth.

Yet the Truth to which they belong, truth according to Christianity, is not the anonymous and impersonal reason of the moderns, nor the empty exteriority of the world where things become visible. This truth is the Truth of Life, the impetus by which it proceeds in itself, springs forth ceaselessly in itself, embracing itself in the First Self in whom, loving itself in him, who loves himself in it, it reveals itself in the profusion and splendor of his Parousia.

Each time a living being comes to life in its timeless birth, this movement is repeated. It is in the Self of absolute Life, in his Word [*Verbe*], that each self is in turn engendered: "In him all was made." Humans belong to the Truth of Life insofar as they are engendered in its Word [*Verbe*]. Whoever, engendered in the Word [*Verbe*], belongs to its Truth, hears the word of God.

The place where someone who comes from God hears the word of God, is the heart. In this place, the hearing of the Word is identical with the generation of the human. There, in the self-revelation of Life in its Word [*Verbe*], the self-revelation is accomplished which makes the human being truly human. Hearing the word is thus consubstantial with human nature. This identity of the revelation of humans to themselves in their heart with the revelation of God in his Word [*Verbe*] explains why God sees the secret of the hearts, one of the great themes of the teaching of Christ addressed to humans. A decisive theme, as we have seen, since it shifts entirely the place where the true human stands, tearing us away from naive representations which situate humans in the world where they are merely empirical individuals subject to the laws of the world, emptied of the passionate interiority which defines their very essence — mere objects, subject to all the reductions to which we are witness today: psychological, sociological, political, biological, physical, and so forth.

Yet this identity of the revelation of the human in his or her heart with the revelation of God in his Word [*Verbe*] is not only the source of the great light shed by the Gospel on human nature; it brings a solution to our final question. *The possibility for humans to hear the word of Christ in their hearts is precisely that of comprehending the Scriptures.* We have just recalled the obstacle this reading encounters. Are the words of Christ, reported to us through the intermediary of written texts, not affected by the doubt which affects any human word, written or oral? Does it not also refer to an external referent whose existence it is incapable of positing?

In the case of the Scriptures, this difficulty increases considerably: here the always more or less problematic referent of human language no longer exists. Those who spoke the words reported in the Gospels, supposing that they really were spoken, have disappeared, their faces having faded into the mists of history. Are not the words of Christ himself which resounded under the sky of Judea and Galilee, arousing the admiration or the rage of his listeners, very far from us, belonging to a vanished world? In still supposing here that they were really spoken as they have come down to us, what relationship is there between the civilization on which they depended and the one in which we live? What meaning can these words still have for us?

Yet, Christ's word which rang out throughout the villages of the Jewish land, in the synagogues of Nazareth and of Capernaum, on the roads of Samaria or under the vaults of the Temple in Jerusalem, is the Word [*Parole*] of the Word [*Verbe*], the Word [*Parole*] in which we have been engendered. In it, our life has come to life; each person is revealed to him-

or herself as being forever this self irreducible to any other. This word speaks in us; it speaks its own life to each one of us. Each one of us hears it. We hear it not as one hears the noise of the world. We hear it in the silence where no noise is possible, no gaze — in the secret of the heart where God sees, where his Word speaks. Each of us hears it in our suffering and in our joy, in our ennui as much as through our Desire which has no object on earth. This Word is not itself our suffering or our joy, but the embrace in which we experience them. In them we suddenly experience this embrace, stronger than ourselves, the limitless power which continually wells up in us and gives us to ourselves. It is, then, the Word of God which we hear.

Yet this Word does not speak only to each one of us in our timeless birth — where, brothers of the Firstborn, Icon of the divine essence, we are given to ourselves in the self-revelation of Life in his Word [*Verbe*]. It is also expressed in human language. And this happened twice in history. It spoke through the prophets, before turning us upside down when it became that of Christ.

It is now easy to understand what is expressed by their voice [that of the prophets]. We have seen that the human word does not speak only of the things of the world, which moreover only have meaning for our life. The human word first speaks of this life. Someone who suffers can always say "I suffer," using this language made up of sounds ("phonemes"), carriers of all the significations taken from his or her own life of which they are only varied representations. The prophets also spoke of life, but they did not speak of it in a naive manner as a set of empirical and dubious "psychic facts." Because the Word of truth which judges the world rumbled at the bottom of their heart, sorrowful before the idolatry of the world, filled with its anger, they hurled at humans their unworthiness.

The Word of Christ is also spoken to humans in their own language, whether it tells them about themselves or about itself. He tells them such strange things about themselves and about him. Yet how can we believe this Word, especially considering its strangeness? How can we know whether what he has said to them is true, or whether it is instead the utterance of someone "possessed"? Let us recall one more time the obstacle against which ordinary language comes up. As long as the propositions that it formulates are plausible and are in accordance with experience, they are credible — without, for all that, being necessarily true. As soon as we have statements contrary to experience or totally bizarre, as are Christ's affirmations about humanity and about himself, doubt and skepticism creep in. Human language refers to content external to itself and is incapable of proving its reality. How can we believe in this reality that it is so implausible and that, additionally, we cannot see?

Christ says to humans: you are the sons of God, "you have only one Father." Where is the referent of this assertion? *In us.* We are sons of God. God is Life and we are living beings. Are there living beings somewhere who do not carry life in themselves, who would not be carried by it? This is not a philosophical and speculative thesis. *We feel and experience life in us as that in which we live, even when we feel and experience that we have not given this life to ourselves.* The self-revelation in which we are given and revealed to ourselves, is the Word [*Parole*] of Life, is its Word [*Verbe*]. Thus we are the irresistible proof of what the Word [*Parole*] says to us, there where it does not cease to speak our own life to us. Whoever hears this Word, where it speaks to us, forever hears the sound of his or her birth in him- or herself. It is to us that the Word says: "Today, I have engendered you" [Heb. 1:5].

The extraordinary agreement established between the word that Christ speaks to humans in their own language and the one which generates all of us in our hearts and speaks our own birth to us, causes an intense emotion in those who recognize it. It is this emotion that the two disciples feel when, overcome by the death and the crucifixion of the one in whom they had placed their hope, they walk along sadly toward the town of Emmaus. They share their dismay with the man who joins them on the dark road and who seems to be completely ignorant of what has happened in Jerusalem. "Then he said to them, 'Oh, how foolish you are, and how slow of heart to believe all that the prophets have declared! Was it not necessary that the Messiah should suffer these things and then enter into his glory?' Then beginning with Moses and all the prophets, he interpreted to them the things about himself in all the scriptures." After they have recognized him at the inn and he has disappeared from their sight, they say to each other, "'Were not our hearts burning within us while he was talking to us on the road, while he was opening the scriptures to us?'" (Luke 24:25-32).

The same principle which allows us to understand the Scriptures is thus the one which legitimates Christ's words about himself: it is for us the Word [*Parole*] of the Word [*Verbe*]. This is the word which dictated to the prophets what they proclaimed to their contemporaries, and gave the Evangelists the texts in which they reported what they heard. The Word [*Parole*] of Christ inasmuch as it is that of the Word [*Verbe*] is hence the only source that opens the understanding of the sacred texts to us. It is the Spirit who simultaneously has produced these texts and who grounds their intelligibility. Only the Spirit permits us to know the Spirit.

This relationship of the sacred text to the Spirit shines forth in the extraordinary event that took place in the synagogue of Nazareth. We know how, receiving the book of Isaiah for the purpose of doing the reading, Christ opens to the following passage: "'The Spirit of the Lord is upon me, because he has anointed me to bring good news to the poor. He has sent me to proclaim release to the captives and recovery of sight to the blind. . . .' And he rolled up the scroll. . . . Then he began to say to them, 'Today this scripture has been fulfilled in your hearing'" (Luke 4:18-21). Here, the referent of language is not aimed at an unreal and problematic signification: *it is here present, being clearly indicated as the Spirit of the Lord.* Nevertheless in this solemn circumstance — "the eyes of all in the synagogue were fixed on him" — one of the first confrontations between Christ and the "Jews" occurs. The clash intensified with Christ's provocative words declaring that Elijah had not been sent to a widow in Israel, but rather to a foreign widow, and that at the time of Elisha no leper was purified in Israel, but only a Syrian — words prefiguring his own fate and that of Christianity, turning toward the Gentiles, recalled in [John's] Prologue, verse 11: "He came to what was his own, and his own people did not accept him."

Why did the inhabitants of Nazareth not recognize him when he came home to them with an aura of fame spread throughout the entire region? They had known the child well, that is true: "no prophet is accepted in his hometown." Is it not, rather, because this recognition occurs in the heart, provided that, escaping from the world and its idols, it remains open to the Word of the Spirit — to this very Word that they have come to hear. We know the explanation given by Christ for human

120

deafness. "Everyone who has heard and learned from the Father comes to me" (John 6:45). "Whoever is from God hears the words of God. The reason you do not hear them is that you are not from God" (John 8:47). Here, in this Johannine context, the reply suggested by Christ in all the Gospels becomes more radical. In the very place of hearing, evil has arisen, disrupting or destroying the constitutive link of the heart, its relationship to the Word. The way in which evil takes the place of the divine origin — to the point of substituting a new principle for it, *a different father* — is the object of Christ's denunciation: "You are from your father the devil, and you choose to do your father's desires. He was a murderer from the beginning and does not stand in the truth, because there is no truth in him. When he lies, he speaks according to his own nature, for he is a liar and the father of lies" (John 8:44). Thus the original generation of humanity in the Word [*Verbe*] is suddenly annihilated, in such a way that the work of divine "creation" is seriously compromised.

Human destiny is therefore at stake in the hearing of the Word: "Then pay attention to how you listen" (Luke 8:18). In true hearing, when accomplished as hearing of the Word, humans are faithful to the gift of God; they surrender themselves to the working of this gift in them, in which they are given to themselves in the self-revelation of life. In some way they have mobilized from this moment what dwells in their hearts as a 'given': this gift.

By contrast, the human condition is turned upside down by the radical egoism which takes itself as the ground of its being and of its action, knowing no other law than its pleasure — than itself — and secretly turning its anxious concern back to the world and its preoccupations. We discount as absolutely nothing the gift of Life in us, this gift which always precedes us. This clarifies these apparently mysterious but rigorous words: "To those who have, more will be given; and from those who do not have, even what they seem to have will be taken away" (Luke 8:18; cf. Mark 4:25; Matt. 13:12).

Those who, having received the gift of Life, have not forgotten it but keep in themselves the Word and listen to it, are thus the ones who do not cease to "bear fruit," increase their riches, receive even more. To them is given the revelation in which the Word consists. In the Synoptic Gospels the context of the astonishing propositions we have just read, namely the parable of the lamp, eliminates any ambiguity: "He said to them: 'Is a lamp brought in to be put under the bushel basket, or under the bed, and not on the lampstand?'" (Mark 4:21). This allows us to hear the grandiose statements in the Logia, of which one recognizes a trace even in the apocrypha. "For nothing is hidden that will not be disclosed, nor is anything secret that will not become known and come to light" (Luke 8:17).

It is important not to forget how the secret comes out into broad daylight, how the revelation is made. The revelation of our finite life in the absolute Life holds all these characteristics within it. It can never be interpreted as knowledge of an object, as an apparition whose light is that of the world. Because this revelation is accomplished as life and therefore in life, it actually penetrates all of life's modalities — especially our action. In tearing away the mask of hypocrisy, has Christ's teaching not established that in its realization the real action escapes from the reign of the visible, developing in the secret of the heart where God sees it? "Coming into broad daylight" means that this invisible light illumines the hearts. The entire Christian ethic assumes that it is not a matter of *speaking* (in the sense of ordinary language), but of *doing*. "Not everyone who says to me, 'Lord, Lord,' will enter the kingdom of heaven, but only the one who does the will of my Father in heaven" (Matt. 7:21).

The Word which speaks to the heart, the Word of Life which has engendered it, is the same which, transforming it from top to bottom, has the power to bring about the regeneration of humans, reestablishing them in the splendor of their original status as sons.

This is the occasion for going back to a proof that Christ gives of his divine status in the debate ceaselessly carried on with the Pharisees, the scribes, and the religious leaders — namely, the identity of his Word [*Parole*] with that of God, an identity which shows him to be the Word [*Verbe*]. A surprising proof because, among all the statements in which Christ gradually unveils *who he is,* this is the only time where he refers to humans as *those who will be able to experience and test in themselves the truth of Christ's word regarding himself.* This text is unusual indeed. "Anyone who resolves to do the will of God will know whether the teaching is from God or whether I am speaking on my own" (John 7:17). What is defined in this essential proposition is the phenomenon of religious experience, an indisputable experience for anyone to whom it is given. And this experience comes to humans each time that, hearing the Word and surrendering themselves to it, they do the will of God. For example, forgetting themselves in the work of mercy and giving themselves entirely to the fulfillment of this commitment, they are no longer distinguishable from it. When their action has thus become the will of the Father, whoever accomplishes it experiences the extraordinary release of a heart delivered from all finitude and of the burden of human egoism. They know that the Word whose paradoxical teaching they follow does not come from a man but from God. Thus they also experience in themselves the truth of Christ's promise: "If you continue in my word, you are truly my disciples; and you will know the truth, and the truth will make you free" (John 8:31-32).

Religious experience, the overwhelming experience of freedom, is thus only given to someone who listens to the Word. Does not listening to the Word, however, assume a pure heart, delivered from evil — from the traumatism and the deceit in which evil has enveloped all things? "If then the light in you is darkness, how great is the darkness!" (Matt. 6:23; cf. Luke 11:35). Is the possibility of religious experience which frees humans not thus caught in a circle? Only hearing the Word can deliver us from evil, but evil has made it impossible to listen to the Word.

The one whose words are reported in the Gospels knew all that. Wanting to save humans by freeing them from the slavery of sin, without doubt he had no other recourse than to proceed forcefully. Since only those who have the original Word of Life at their disposal in their hearts will be able to hear it, to listen to it, to remain faithful to it, and thus to be saved, is it not necessary that this Word would come among us in order to give itself to us? The Incarnation of the Word [*Verbe*] in the flesh of Christ is this coming of the Word [*Parole*] of Life into a flesh like ours. Henceforth, for this Word [*Parole*] of God to be actually received by us, the condition is that Christ give us his own flesh which is that of the Word [*Verbe*] — which he gives to us in his flesh, uniting his flesh to ours, in such a way that it would be in us and we in him — in the same way as he is in the Father and the Father is in him.

Is it not a bit presumptuous to elaborate such reflections about God's purposes? Paul will ask: Who has been his counselor? [Rom. 11:34]

Nevertheless, Christ himself made revelations of this sort in the synagogue at Capernaum: "I am the bread of life. Your ancestors ate the manna in the wilderness and they died. This is the bread that comes down from heaven, so that one may eat of it and not die. I am the living bread that came down from heaven. Whoever eats of this bread will live forever; and the bread that I will give for the life of the world is my flesh." The Jews discussed among themselves: "How can this man give us his flesh to eat?" Jesus said to them then: "Very truly, I tell you, unless you eat the flesh of the Son of Man and drink his blood, you have no life in you. . . . Those who eat my flesh and drink my blood abide in me, and I in them. Just as the living Father sent me, and I live because of the Father, so whoever eats me will live because of me" (John 6:47-57).

These words, which scandalized so many of his disciples, are no longer those of instruction but of salvation. They offer us the opportunity for a final reflection on the Word. God's Word is opposed to the human word which, when it is not actually deceptive, is more than limited in power. Our word carries the mark of finitude even more than our action. The tyrant or dictator or president who says: "The court is now in session," and whom one obeys without objection, might be overthrown by tomorrow by those who bow down before him or her today — and who in turn will experience the same fate.

In contrast, the omnipotence of the divine Word is that of absolute Life. The institution of the Eucharist which the Synoptic Gospels report exhibits this power: "This is my body." During the unbroken memorial of this institution across the centuries, Christ's sovereign word, repeated by the priest, consecrates the offering.

The economy of salvation is shown in all clarity in Capernaum. The omnipotence of the Word [*Parole*] is the invincible coming into itself of absolute Life, revealing itself in its Word [*Verbe*]. Because the Word [*Verbe*] has become incarnate in Christ's flesh, the identification with this flesh is the identification with the Word [*Verbe*] — to eternal Life. "Those who eat my flesh and drink my blood have eternal life, and I will raise them up on the last day" (John 6:54).